Keep Taking
the Tablets

Keep Taking the Tablets

*A Prescriptive Guide to the
Ten Commandments*

David Carr

New Wine Press

New Wine Ministries
PO Box 17
Chichester
West Sussex
United Kingdom
PO19 2AW

ISBN 978–1–903725–87–0

Typeset by CRB Associates, Reepham, Norfolk
Cover design by CCD, www.ccdgroup.co.uk
Printed in Malta

Contents

Introduction

During the year of 2006 I preached a series of sermons with the title: "The Laws of the Kingdom". What was initially planned as a four week study turned into a series that lasted thirty-two weeks in total! Having embarked on a discussion about the Old Testament Law and its relevance for us today, I could see it was having a real impact on people and they were hungry for more, so I continued. I often feel deep admiration for the people whom I serve as Senior Pastor! In fact, I stand in amazement as the crowds grow each week. Praise God for all He is doing!

This book focuses on the latter part of that teaching series when I got around to tackling the Ten Commandments, which we may consider to be the very heart of the Law as they are not so much a list of rules as a reflection of God's character. But more on that later. For now it will be helpful for the reader to have a brief overview of the background to God's unveiling of the Commandments.

Every nation, society and community exists by observing certain laws. Laws make up the framework in which these social groupings can exist. Once established, the law is the law – regardless of political expression, cultural influence or religious belief. The law is necessary because without any prescribed direction people would live in chaos.

So it was for the children of Israel, God's people. Many laws governed their daily lives and these were grouped into three main categories:

- Ceremonial
- Civic
- Moral

1. The ceremonial law

This centred around the worship of Almighty God. The ceremonial law specified and directed every aspect of the regular sacrifices that were made, the workings of the Tabernacle and Temple, the function of the Levitical Priesthood and High Priest, the design of the Tabernacle and Temple furniture, including the ark of the Covenant, and the various acts associated with Temple worship.

All these functions and objects held prophetic meaning and, when studied, they unwrap a beautiful template for our worship and praise of God today. Children need instruction – the children of Israel needed to be taught how to worship God and so do we. We tend to view worship as a purely personal and private affair, yet whilst it has that aspect, the worship of God has always been and should always be a corporate expression as Scripture confirms in numerous places. When the church gathers together each of us is called to bring a psalm, a hymn or a spiritual song, making melody in our hearts to the Lord. Worship is both individual and corporate and it is the church's responsibility to teach and model worship as a way of life.

The Lord is still seeking those who will worship Him in Spirit and in truth. Our expression of worship to God enables us to see ourselves, others, and our society in a true light, with a truly Christian perspective.

The Bible says that, *"righteousness exalts a nation"* (Proverbs 14:34). It was the ceremonial law that kept Israel at the cutting edge of its day. The worship of Almighty God laid the foundations for the building of a true house of "Prayer Praise". It was true for the nation and for the individual that "seeking first the Kingdom of God" lay at the heart of Israel's life and the result was amazing blessing and prosperity as God was honoured and revered.

2. The civic law

The civic law was the agreed system of government and administration. It dictated education, health, fiscal policies, business ethics and the general infrastructure of society. Israel had very precise instructions on how to rule and administer the law for the benefit of the whole community. It created a "corporate goodwill" and gave society the ability to trade and develop prosperity. Flanked by the ceremonial and moral law, civic law kept business and political life clean and focused. Jesus, quoting the Old Testament, reminded us that life is about more than "bread": *"Man shall not live by bread alone but by every word that proceeds out of the mouth of God."* Yet the civil law was God's vehicle for enabling His people to receive provision and to enable each person to contribute to their community.

Both Jews and Muslims extend their faith and beliefs into their civic law. We hear a great deal these days about "Sharia Law" – a defined outworking of Islamic law that controls all aspects of legal and business activity. "Sharia" means "way" or "path" and provides the framework within which public and some private aspects of a Muslim's life are regulated. It becomes their daily living. Christians in the West have no such prescribed tenets, yet our spiritual reality should stand for effective government, justice and the oversight of the environment. Scripture encourages us to, *"pray for those who have rule over you that you may have a peaceable life."*

3. The moral law

It was as I started to address this third category of law, the Ten Commandments, that I received a fresh insight into the oldest, yet most used, moral code in history, insight that I hope will prove useful to you as you read this book. A great deal of teaching and preaching over the years has been given over to the content of the two tablets given by God to Moses, on which the Ten Commandments were inscribed by His own finger. Yet in our present-day society, which is fast becoming a moral vacuum, very few are aware of what the Commandments actually say. Fewer still would seek to live by them. Most people seem to regard them as outdated and irrelevant to life as we know it. Even Christians tend to believe that the Old Testament laws do not have the same weight of authority now we are "living under grace".

Do I really believe that? Yes! We know very well that most of the Commandments are broken on a daily basis by those who do not subscribe to them, but as a Pastor I have seen, increasingly, among Christians and Christian leaders that many are living a lifestyle that puts self-gratification before covenant. God's moral laws have become easier to violate since we have become desensitised to the spiritual and moral discipline that characterizes a truly Spirit-filled life. However, I am not setting out to bash people over the head with those facts. I believe many readers will be challenged, yet inspired by the fresh approach in this book.

Far from being irrelevant to us today, Jesus spoke about the Ten Commandments and taught that it was possible to fulfil them all through love. Truly loving God, yourself and your neighbour, Jesus said, is the key to ensuring we keep His moral law. The law centres on relationship. To break a commandment always brings us into conflict with God, ourselves and others. Each one of the Commandments covers some aspect of this three-fold relationship. If the *agape* love of God rests upon and within us we will know a responsive affection for the Lord, self-acceptance, and a deep respect for others. If that is the case then we will naturally not want to offend God, defile our own righteousness, or destroy the sanctity of others.

It is the love of God in Christ Jesus that opens the door for the Ten Commandments to be the active morality that reveals the nature and heart of Almighty God. In other words, they are far more than a set of rules and regulations. They are more revelatory than regulatory! They reveal God's nature to us. One commandment says, "Do not commit adultery." What does that reveal to us about God? He values faithfulness and intimacy. His love never violates others and He wants us to love in the same way. God's love is based on giving, not taking what belongs to someone else. John 3:16 speaks of God so loving the world that He gave His only begotten Son – now that's love! Love is sacrificial. True love is not seeking personal gratification at the expense of others – that is the basis of lust, not love.

Keep taking the tablets

Isaiah prophesied that Jesus would come to show us the favour of the Lord; to declare the year of Jubilee for all mankind – an era of freedom from the past and prosperity for the future. And this is precisely what He did through His death, resurrection, ascension, and the gift of the Holy Spirit. Yet, for all that, Jesus did not come to abolish the Law, but uphold it, and He said so explicitly. Grace is always "more than" the Law. Where the Law established a principle, grace takes it to a higher level.

God's intention is that through grace we now live in the Ten Commandments not under them. Notice that I say "in them", not "above them" or "under them". No Christian lives above the law of God and no Christian lives under the law of God. Rather we live "inside" these life-giving, life-preserving statutes. It is possible for every Christian to love God with all their hearts; to live free from idolatry. What makes it eminently possible is the fact that we now have the power of the Holy Spirit living and breathing within us.

The title of this book, *Keep Taking the Tablets*, is novel and a play on words. Or is it? We all know that the Ten Commandments were written on stone tablets. Modern culture, however, has spawned a pill-popping generation where many are looking for relief from pain or a path to wholeness by taking prescribed medicine. The doctor will say to us, "Take one, three times a day." We aren't cured by a single pill, but by taking a consistent dosage over a period of time. So it is with God's moral law. "Taking the tablets" is not a one-off, once for all immunisation against the sinful nature. As Paul put it, we have to "die daily" to self to maintain a righteous, holy "fitness" for life.

Since September 2, 1987, when I had a heart attack, I have

taken one 75ml dissolvable aspirin every day to keep my blood thin. What effect is that having on me? Well, when I had dental treatment recently the dentist and his assistant struggled to stop the bleeding! We don't always see the effect of what goes on inside us, but others do! As you read the Commandments on these tablets allow them to "dissolve" into your mind and spirit and you will be transformed from the inside out. Think of the Commandments not as a list of prohibitions, but of possibilities. We can do all things through Christ who strengthens us. These Commandments are not wishful thinking for a few, but *wilful* thinking for all.

You may well ask at this point, "David, can I really be expected to keep the Commandments? People didn't in the Old Testament." Correct, but Jesus Christ came to fulfil what man could not. He brought completion to the Old Covenant and then, through His gift of the Holy Spirit, released to us the ability to experience the richness of New Covenant life. Ask yourself this question: "If the Commandments cannot be kept, which one of the ten would you allow your Minister or Elder to break and turn a blind eye?" Murder? Worshipping a graven image? Bearing false witness? Committing adultery? No, you expect them to live a high moral and spiritual life and rightly so. But, if they can keep God's law, so can you!

I trust as you read this book and reflect on its teaching you will linger at the end of each commandment giving thanks to a God who loves us enough to give us the guidance to live a full and blessed life. Remember what the doctor said to you when you last saw him: "Keep taking the tablets."

The Giving of the Ten Commandments

Before God announced the Ten Commandments to Moses and, via him, to the people of Israel He took the time to remind the people what He had already done for them. He did this because it's hard to respond to God unless you know who He is and what He's done for you – just like someone hearing the Gospel for the very first time. God is wonderful because He does things for us before we know Him and then reveals to us what He has done. That act in itself helps us to know Him!

What had God done for the people that He wanted to remind them about? There were three things: He had brought them out of Egypt, brought them out of oppression, and brought them out of slavery. This was just the tip of the iceberg in terms of what God wanted to do for His people. He had so much more that He wanted to do for them. But in between what God had done and what He would do, came the signing of a covenant – the agreement of the Ten Commandments. God was calling His people to come closer to Him and enter into a contract. This is what He promised:

> *"Now therefore, if you will indeed obey My voice and keep My covenant, then you shall be a special treasure to Me above all people; for all the earth is Mine."* (Exodus 19:5)

The two key statements that Israel needed to hear were "Obey My voice" and "Keep My covenant." Over one hundred times in Scripture we are told to obey God. 1 Samuel 15:22 is a classic example:

> *"Has the Lord as great delight in burnt offerings and*
> * sacrifices,*
> *As in obeying the voice of the Lord?*
> *Behold, to obey is better than sacrifice,*
> *And to heed than the fat of rams."*

Again we read in Deuteronomy 4:30–31,

> *"When you are in distress, and all these things come upon you in the latter days, when you turn to the Lord your God and obey His voice (for the Lord your God is a merciful God), He will not forsake you nor destroy you, nor forget the covenant of your fathers which He swore to them."*

God's message to His people was simple: why sin and have to pay penance for it, when obedience will save the pain of restoration? God in His kindness was helping people to see that obedience to His commands (which are designed for our good and are to our benefit) is a higher way than an endless cycle of sin and repentance.

Many people have a problem with this word "obey" because, I believe, they misunderstand its meaning. The Hebrew for the word "obey" does not mean, as most people take it, "Do what I tell you and do it NOW!" We tend to view obedience in the same way as a frustrated parent with wayward children does. Because they cannot tolerate any more bad behaviour they seek to stamp down their authority and demand compliance, or else their kids will suffer the consequences. How many parents, when their children question an order and ask "Why?" will simply respond, "Because I'm telling you to!"?

God is not like that. He has never been like that. God never commands that we do something and says, if we question it, "Because I say so!" God is a relational God and He tells us things because He wants us to live life to the full, receiving every benefit from Him we possibly can. God's desire is to tell us things that will bless us. The trouble is, we're not very good at listening!

So when God says, "Obey Me" it is not because He is autocratic. The form of the Hebrew phrase "to obey" actually means "to hear intelligently". In other words God says to us, "I want you to obey Me because you understand and love Me." He wants us to realize that obedience releases the riches of His blessings upon us. The root word also means "to give consent; to be diligent; to discern and to perceive".

God then, in His introduction to the Ten Commandments, wanted His people to understand His heart of love towards them and to perceive that His covenant was designed to bring about wholeness, fulfilment and blessing in their lives. He refers to Himself as the God who saves them, and He also wants to save them from the pain and suffering that living outside of His code for life would bring. How amazing! God doesn't just lay down the law – He wants His people to understand the need for obedience and the benefits it will bring. That is relationship.

It is important to realize that at this point the average person had no direct relationship with God. God spoke to His specially commissioned servants direct, but apart from to these people – such as Moses – God was generally unknown and mysterious. The people hadn't got a clue about what He was really like – and this, as we will see, was one of the key reasons that He gave them the Ten Commandments. However, God has always wanted to bring people into closer relationship with Himself; to understand what He is like; and this is what He was offering the people as He revealed the Ten Commandments.

The Ten Commandments stood in between freedom from the past – Egypt – and the freedom of the future as God promised to make them a "special treasure". Obedience would be the key to future blessing. How many reading this feel that they have the potential to do great things for God; that they have a specific destiny carved out for them by Him? Simple obedience will be the key to achieving it. Mostly God does not give us great Damascus road type experiences to set us on course for our destiny; He just wants us to obey Him step by step. Campbell McAlpine said, "In life there are very few crossroads of decision, but many milestones of obedience."

God desires that we know His heart and in doing so, allow ourselves to be immersed in Him, becoming ever more like Him. God's nature is love and His commandments are rooted in and centred upon that love. If we are soaking in the love of God then, actually, keeping the Ten Commandments will become second nature to us. Obedience to them will be just as much a part of our nature as it is God's. When we realize this, the Ten Commandments become less of a set of rules and more of a benediction from God, spoken over us to bless us.

God wanted to reveal to the people exactly what He was like

– a God who was not adulterous, but ever faithful, a God who was holy and just. His desire was that when the people saw what He was like they would want to be like Him – and in so doing they would be rescued from sin and misery and become all that He intended them to be. The Ten Commandments were not intended to judge the people, but to inspire them to righteousness.

The covenant

Just like a man and woman who, when they marry, make a covenantal agreement, so God, in order to fulfil His promise of future blessing for His people, required them to make a covenant with Him. God's covenant with His people was very much like a marriage with God as the bridegroom and His people as the bride. When a woman gets married, she signs the marriage register with her maiden name for the very last time. The husband signs his name and thereafter the wife takes on her husband's name, identifying herself with him and the covenant they have made together. The deal with the covenant is: you come as you are and you leave as one, joined together.

This is what God wanted for His people. God had already declared His promises for His people. In other words, He had already said, "I will." Now it was the people's turn to sign on the dotted line. They needed to confess their part of the covenant or it could not become absolute. When Moses came down from the mountain and told the people all about what God had said, they responded by saying, "All that the Lord has spoken, we will do." At that moment the covenant was fixed.

But despite the fact that they readily entered into the covenant with God, unfortunately the people were not obedient.

In fact, they more or less immediately forgot what they had signed up to and went their own way, turning their backs on God's goodness. Astonishing! Because of this, God ended up giving the commandments twice.

Initially the commandments were a positive proclamation intended to encourage the people to righteousness living by revealing the kind of God they served. It was an opportunity to enjoy the intimacy and protection of a covenant relationship with God. But, while Moses was on the mountain conversing with God and the Lord was in the very act of transcribing His commandments onto the stone tablets with His own finger, the people were busy sinning.

> *"When the people saw that Moses was so long in coming down from the mountain, they gathered around Aaron and said, 'Come, make us gods who will go before us. As for this fellow Moses who brought us up out of Egypt, we don't know what has happened to him."* (Exodus 32:1, NIV)

God, realizing what was taking place, told Moses,

> *"Go down, because your people, whom you brought up out of Egypt, have become corrupt. They have been quick to turn away from what I commanded them and have made themselves an idol cast in the shape of a calf. They have bowed down to it and sacrificed to it and have said, 'These are your gods, O Israel, who brought you up out of Egypt.'"* (Exodus 32:7–8, NIV)

Literally as God was writing the people turned away and fell headlong into idolatry. Even Aaron, Moses' brother, who had been so mightily used of God immediately slipped into the deception and went along with it. He had been by Moses' side all along and God had blessed him and made him a priest, yet here he was committing a gross sin. Notice the subtlety of the language God uses here. It was, of course, God who had delivered the people and led them out of Egypt, and yet He says, *"**Your** people, whom **you** brought up out of Egypt, have become corrupt."* God was disowning them.

Naturally, God was very angry. In fact He wanted to destroy Israel, He was so angry, and start again with Moses. But, Moses persuaded God to relent and not bring disaster on the people. Then Moses went back down the mountain carrying the two stone tablets to confront the people. We are told,

> *"When Moses approached the camp and saw the calf and the dancing, his anger burned and he threw the tablets out of his hands, breaking them to pieces at the foot of the mountain. And he took the calf they had made and burned it in the fire; then he ground it to powder, scattered it on the water and made the Israelites drink it."*   (Exodus 32:19–20, NIV)

What do you think caused the people of Israel to turn from God so quickly? God had liberated Israel from Egypt and was taking them on a journey to the Promised Land. They were God-worshipping people, yet they had a weakness. Their weakness was this: they had come out of Egypt, but Egypt had not come out of them. As soon as they were put under a bit of pressure they began whinging and asking to go back to Egypt – back into slavery! It's astonishing that they would prefer a life of servitude to cruel taskmasters than a life of freedom serving Almighty God, but that is what they asked for. Then, the minute Moses turned his back, they were creating a golden calf!

Still relevant today?

At this point you might say, "This is a great history lesson David, but how is all this relevant to Christianity today?" There has been a tendency among Charismatic Christians to dismiss much of the content of the Old Testament as irrelevant since we are now "living under the New Covenant" in Christ. In the broadest terms this has meant that many have rejected what they see as outmoded practices belonging to the Mosaic Law – including tithing amongst other things. In this book we are concerning ourselves with the modern-day relevance of the Ten Commandments. Whilst most Christians agree that we should uphold these ten fundamental rules for life, I have encountered a widespread ignorance – among new Christians particularly – concerning what they actually say and mean in practice. There is also, it seems to me, a sad lack of determination to uphold them among mature Christians who should know better.

A particular stumbling block for many is the distinction between what is Law and legalism. When we talk about something being *legalistic*, our spiritual alarm bells immediately begin ringing, because we understand that legalism belongs to dead religious ritual, whilst we are called to life in the Spirit. However, Christians tend to tar God's Law with the same brush. There is a difference! Believers living under the New Covenant are still called to uphold God's Law and that is why the Ten Commandments are relevant to us today. Law is something that is given by God and is fulfilled in Him. Legalism is our flawed human interpretation of God's Law and represents our attempts to respond to it and keep it.

Luke 18:18–20 provides one of the clearest examples in Scripture of how and why we should continue to observe and uphold the Ten Commandments. In His encounter with a rich young ruler who was looking for answers, Jesus gave a response which is insightful for us. He immediately quoted several key commandments:

> *"Now a certain ruler asked Him, saying, 'Good Teacher, what shall I do to inherit eternal life?'*
>
> *So Jesus said to him, 'Why do you call Me good? No one is good but One, that is, God. You know the commandments: "Do not commit adultery," "Do not murder," "Do not steal," "Do not bear false witness," "Honour your father and your mother."'"*

Immediately we can see that Jesus is upholding the Law. He keeps it simple, saying, "You know as well as I do what's written in the Law." But let's take a closer look at these verses, because they throw up a number of issues that are important to understand.

Firstly, it is worth noting that Jesus alludes to His deity in His response. He says to the young man, "You call me good, but only God is good." In other words, "Do you realize you are calling me God?" Jesus then goes on to speak out several of the commandments to the man. Only God can give commandments and only He can truly fulfil them. Only God has the right to judge people on the basis of the commandments. So, in effect, Jesus was asserting His right to do this and confirming His identity as the Son of God, co-equal with the Father. This is the truth that every cult denies.

Secondly, we notice that the young man came to Jesus looking for *eternal life*. He is described as being "rich" so I think it is safe to assume that he had just about everything life could offer him. However, he knew that he lacked something important – an assurance of eternal wellbeing. No matter how many material possessions we accumulate in this life, in the end there is only one thing we will really care about – where and how we are going to spend eternity.

We are also told that this man was "young". He wasn't an old man, faced with his own mortality, who had begun thinking, "I'd better get my life sorted out." He was a young man who simply wanted to know, "What must I do to inherit eternal life?" This was a great question to ask and the young man's phrasing is interesting. It showed that he had grasped one important factor, but had misunderstood another. He had at least understood that eternal life had to be "inherited". But he asks, "What must I *do* . . . ?" The fact is, we cannot do anything to inherit eternal life. It cannot be earned or purchased. If that were possible, no doubt the young man would have already bought it – he had plenty of money. Just as when a relative dies and leaves you money in their will, you inherit something, so the inheritance of eternal life comes out of relationship. It is your connection with a particular person that brings inheritance about. In the same way our eternal inheritance comes via our relationship with the Father through Jesus.

On another occasion, Jesus was asked the same question, but this time by "an expert in the law". The New King James Version actually describes this man as "a lawyer". This time Jesus doesn't respond to the question directly, perhaps because of this man's profession, and instead, He answers the question with a question:

> " 'What is written in the law? What is your reading of it?'
> So he answered and said, 'You shall love the LORD your God
> with all your heart, with all your soul, with all your strength,

and with all your mind,' and 'your neighbour as yourself.' And
He said to him, 'You have answered rightly; do this and you will
live.'"   (Luke 10:26–28)

Here Jesus points to the fact that the commandments can be
summed up by two pre-eminent commandments that encapsul-
ate the rest: if you love God with all your being and your fellow
man as much as yourself, you are not going to go wrong. This,
Jesus says, is what a life complete in Him looks like. In Romans
13:9–10 Paul says the same thing:

> *"For the commandments, 'You shall not commit adultery,'*
> *'You shall not murder,' 'You shall not steal,' 'You shall not bear*
> *false witness,' 'You shall not covet,' and if there is any other*
> *commandment, are all summed up in this saying, namely, 'You*
> *shall love your neighbour as yourself.' Love does no harm to a*
> *neighbour; therefore love is the fulfilment of the law."*

So, rather than saying the Law has passed away and the Ten
Commandments are no longer applicable, Paul says these
commandments *must* be fulfilled – and they are fulfilled in love.
One thing that both Jesus and Paul pointed out was that if you
have the ability to love your neighbour then you will be able to
keep all the other commandments – and in order to love your
neighbour you first have to love yourself. Taking a further step
backwards: in order to truly love yourself you must first love
God with all your heart, mind, soul and strength. Can you grasp
the equation that Jesus is putting forward? If you live focused on
Him, with Christ at the centre of your life, you are held in the
bond of love and the liberty of grace. In that position there is
not a commandment you cannot keep.

So keeping the Ten Commandments is essential for living a godly life, but under the New Covenant we think less in terms of ten individual commandments and more in terms of love and grace encompassing them all. New Testament believers now have the ability, through the power of the Holy Spirit, to do what the people of Israel never managed to do – keep God's Law!

I don't get out of bed in the morning thinking to myself, "Oh dear, I wonder if I'm going to bear false witness today?" If you are abiding in Christ then your "Yes" is "Yes" and your "No" is "No". Plus, you don't talk about people behind their back because you are governed by love. If you remain in Christ then you don't have to worry about breaking the commandment. In other words, living connected to Christ and moving in His love and grace will protect you.

Similarly, if you meet a beautiful woman or a handsome man at a party, but realize that your sexuality is secure because you are abiding in God's love and your marriage covenant is safe in His hands, then you can simply acknowledge that this is a lovely looking person and move on. You don't have to fear that by the end of the evening you will end up in bed with them.

In short, if you focus on loving God more than anything else in your life, then many of the issues that trip people up will not be issues for you. You won't have to think twice about whether you love your work or material things more than God. Without wishing to oversimplify matters or trivialise anyone's personal situation, more often than not when a person is struggling with an issue it is because God is not occupying the primary position in their life. It is when other concerns overtake the overriding priority of abiding in Christ and loving God that things begin to go wrong.

You Shall Have No Other Gods Before Me

"You shall have no other gods before Me."
(Exodus 20:3)

Being God-focused

Each of the first four commandments, of which this the first, are concerned with giving God the honour and respect due to His name. These commandments are God-focused, while the remaining six are concerned with humanity's treatment of one another. Someone might well ask the question, "Why does God insist on being honoured? Is it because He is insecure or childish? Isn't it very overbearing of God to *demand* to be worshipped in this way?" But such a view overlooks one singularly important principle – the truth that *all* of the Ten Commandments were conceived by God for our good. Even the first four commandments, which seem to be chiefly for God's benefit when viewed superficially, are actually there for our benefit too. The whole point of the first four commandments, and this commandment in particular, is that being God-focused in life will reap huge rewards and untold benefits. Conversely, focusing on things other than God will reap its own consequences and subsequent "rewards".

The lack of fulfilment in the lives of people outside of Christ has caused society to become increasingly pluralistic. We now live in a culture where people will try anything and everything, apart from God, to bring satisfaction to their life. Commentators often point to this as a characteristic of postmodern society, but this commandment tells us that, in fact, the problem is not a new one but an age-old one. God foresaw that mankind would go down all manner of avenues seeking satisfaction when the answer is actually to seek Him.

The apostle Paul noticed the same kind of pluralism as he walked around Athens and saw the pantheon of gods the people there worshipped. The Greeks had invented gods to represent every facet of life and to assuage all their fears and needs. Yet, they still lacked the knowledge of the One, all-embracing, all-encompassing God. They were cast adrift on a sea of obscure religious ritual that led them nowhere.

Our lives are similarly adrift if we do not know the fullness of God. Just like the Athenians and every culture that preceded them in civilisation, if we do not follow or seek the God of creation then we create all manner of other gods for ourselves. In essence these gods differ very little from the gods of our ancestors – we just have different names or concepts for them. Modern society worships the gods of work, of sex, of drink or drugs, of money, of entertainment. What Man is doing is worshipping the gods he believes will meet his needs – those that will fulfil him in certain ways on certain days as his emotions dictate. Outside of the knowledge of God, that is how the average person lives – and we are meant to be part of a sophisticated, intellectual society!

In Old Testament times the idolatry one reads about appeared to be blatant in its execution. Today idolatry is much more subtly executed and harder to spot. When we are confronted with worshipping an elephant-headed god or a Buddha, idolatry is easy to spot! But an obsession with surfing the Internet that sucks up all your time and alienates you from God and your family is harder to categorise. Yet, it can just as easily be an idol that needs tearing down.

Idolatry occurs whenever we fail to understand that only God will meet all of our needs and we look to a multitude of little gods for relief but never find it. God is the all-sufficient One and the only One who can meet our every need. When we don't understand that we are motivated to look in numerous other directions. When satisfaction is not found by pursuing these other directions, then we search yet more avenues for relief and the cycle is perpetuated. This is why a person who is a drug addict may also be an alcoholic or may have other compulsive-obsessive tendencies. This is why a person who is a millionaire won't be satisfied with one million, or ten million for that matter, and continues to be a workaholic. This is why a person who is promoted at work will not be satisfied until they cannot be promoted any further. It is our deficiency in putting God first and honouring Him above all else that perpetuates such behaviour.

We must note that God always gives us a choice to obey Him or not. He never forces us to do anything against our will. Instead He makes it clear that if we obey Him we will be blessed and if we don't we'll have to own the consequences. In this commandment God is not saying, "You have *got to* have Me as your only God." He is saying something far more important and fundamental than that. The point God is making is that we *cannot* have other gods and Him as well. There is no room for us to worship other gods and to then "bolt on" a relationship with the Almighty. God says, "That cannot be" and, in effect, if we insist on having idols in our life then we neutralise what God is able to do for us.

God is described as "a jealous God", but it isn't jealousy as we understand it in human terms. God is not acting like a spoilt child and saying, "I won't share you with anyone else." He is actually saying, "Do you realize that you will only truly experience my power when you allow Me full access to your life? Until you do that, I am limited." God has no limitations in terms of what He can do, in terms of His potency, but we can "limit" Him in the sense that we prevent Him from working in our life if we refuse to honour Him as the first four commandments stipulate. Remember that Jesus was limited in His ministry by a lack of honour:

> *"They were offended at Him. But Jesus said to them, 'A prophet is not without honour except in his own country and in his own house.' Now He did not do many mighty works there because of their unbelief."*   (Matthew 13:57–58)

Jesus was "limited" because the people of His home town treated Him with contempt. It was a lack of honour that produced the contempt and therefore He was prevented from revealing the fullness of who He was.

So God is not jealous in the sense of being churlish, but He wants us to have an undivided heart towards Him so that we, by our actions, will not limit the blessing He is able to pour out on us. Imagine a husband who told his wife, "You're not fulfilling all my needs, so I have one or two other women on the side." Any wife with an ounce of dignity would kick him out on his ear saying, "You're supposed to be married to me. I'm not sharing you around!" Neither will God share us with false gods because He is utterly devoted to us.

What's your idol?

An honest examination of your life and its habits will probably reveal some degree of idolatry. As already stated – it can be subtle. We often do things as part of our lifestyle that we take for granted and don't think about too much, but could we be being idolatrous? A simple definition of idolatry is putting other things before our relationship with God. Ask yourself, "What are the things in my life that consume the majority of my time, energy and finance?"

It could be something seemingly innocuous like a pastime or a sport. It would not be exaggeration to say that some people are so hooked on football, for instance, that they will put their allegiance to the game before God. I have come across many people who have great difficulty in deciding whether they should go to church or go to a match – and often the match wins. If there is a game on the TV and a prayer meeting on at church, guess which one wins?

I believe football is one of the biggest false gods there is and I speak from experience. As a kid I was totally obsessed with it. I couldn't read and write until I was eighteen, but I could tell you every one of the ninety-two football clubs, where they played, what their nickname was, what colour their kit was (and their away kit!) because it was like a religion to me. I collected every possible footballing magazine I could get my hands on, even if I couldn't read them properly.

But when I gave my life to Christ, God asked me one day, "Do you love Me more than football?" and I said, "Yes." I went upstairs and gathered up my entire collection of wonderful, pristine magazines, collected over many years, took them down to the bottom of the garden and burnt the lot in case I was ever drawn back to them.

Other people will put other things before God in their life, perhaps without realizing they are doing so. They have "other gods" that interfere with their relationship with the Father. It could be that they are "addicted" to a particular TV soap that deep down they know isn't adding anything to their walk with God and often detracts from time they should be spending with Him. It could be that they are absorbed in their business, pouring all their efforts into running it whilst God gets whatever is left. What amazes me is that people behave like this and then say things like, "God is not blessing me. I'm in difficulty with my business . . . my relationships . . . my marriage etc. . . . and I can't understand it!"

There is nothing intrinsically wrong with any of the things I have mentioned, of course, but if they are diminishing your relationship with God and taking up all your time then they have become idols. If other concerns are crowding God out of your life then it's no wonder that He is limited in how He can bless you. There are no grey areas with God. He says to us, "I'm either all God to you or I'm not God at all."

The effects of idolatry

Because we live in a culture steeped in self-seeking idolatry, the average Christian is just as susceptible to it as the unbeliever. I believe this has had a dramatic, negative impact on the effectiveness of the Church in our nation. 1 Samuel 3 demonstrates the effect of idolatry on a nation. In this passage we see two main results of Israel's rejection of God's rulership:

1. The word of the Lord was rare in those days
2. Visions were infrequent

The first consequence of not putting God first is that we lose our ability to hear His voice, to understand what He is saying, and to communicate His heart to others.

In an average week I am privileged to visit churches of many different denominations and to meet with numbers of church leaders. One thing that regularly shocks me is that the Word of God is preached so little in the churches of our nation. In the average church you are more likely to hear a little homily, a few thoughts, or a time of "sharing", rather than a full-blooded Gospel message or an exposition and application of a passage of Scripture. The trend has become to deliver something short that won't keep people away from the TV or golf course for too long! It seems to me that we have placed too much emphasis on building church around the lifestyle of the people, as if the people who come to church are no more than consumers who might pursue other options if they don't like what we are offering. In some circles "Seeker friendly" has come to mean "Don't put yourself out, let us put ourselves out! We don't want you to think that Christianity makes too many demands on you!" Some sections of the Church are so concerned with not putting people off Church that they water down their Christianity and dilute the Gospel. Modern Church is then reduced to, "Say 'Praise the Lord' occasionally and come to the cheese and wine party and you're in!" What we are doing, I believe, is blunting the sharp edge of the Word of God that would cut into people's hearts and expose their sin and their need of a Saviour. Our idolatry is nullifying the word of the Lord.

The second consequence of idolatry is a lack of vision. The context of the 1 Samuel passage refers to a "waking vision" i.e. an encounter with God where revelation is imparted. Similarly, there is a woeful lack of vision, of revelation, amongst church leaders today. Regularly, as leaders come and sit with me in my office, I will ask them, "So, what's your vision?" You might think that is a simple enough question, yet it is alarming how many look at me blankly and respond, "What do you mean?" The fact is, there are many well-meaning individuals with good hearts running churches, but with a distinct lack of vision and direction.

The situation was so bad in Samuel's day that he, a mere boy, was placed in God's temple and became the vessel through whom God spoke to the nation. Eli, the high priest whose job it was to represent the people to God and vice versa had, according to the account of Scripture, totally lost the plot. He was blind as a bat and as dumb as an ox! Eli had fallen for the big lie of idolatry – that you can take your eyes off God, behave however you want, and somehow everything will turn out OK. But in the very next chapter of 1 Samuel we read of a string of disasters taking place – all because there was no revelation from God in the land.

Israel were warring against the Philistines and were being routed by them. They could not understand why they were being defeated by the Philistine army and someone had an idea:

"Why did the LORD bring defeat upon us today before the Philistines? Let us bring the ark of the LORD's covenant from

Shiloh, so that it may go with us and save us from the hand of
our enemies."   (1 Samuel 4:3, NIV)

The ark of God was brought from Shiloh by Eli's sons, Hophni
and Phinehas, to where the Israelite army was camped. This
encouraged the troops greatly, but when they resumed the
battle they suffered horrendous losses – thirty thousand foot
soldiers were slaughtered – Eli's sons were killed and the ark of
God was captured! Things could scarcely have gone worse for
them. Eli, upon hearing the news, was so shocked that he fell
backwards off his chair, broke his neck and died on the spot.
Eli's daughter-in-law, the wife of Phinehas, was pregnant at the
time and she was so shocked that she went into labour and gave
birth prematurely. She died in childbirth but managed to name
her son before she died. She called him "Ichabod" which means
"the glory has departed" and said these words:

"The glory has departed from Israel, for the ark of God has been
captured."   (1 Samuel 4:22)

What a chillingly accurate diagnosis of the situation. Because
the people's idolatry had caused a lack of revelation from God,
His glory had departed. Israel carried on as normal, believing
that because they had found favour in God's sight in the
past, in spite of their double-mindedness and hardness of heart
God would turn up and give them the victory. They were
wrong!

We must never presume on God. God's heart is always to
bless us, but we cannot assume He will keep on blessing us
when we are not careful to put Him first in our life. The
Israelites thought that just because they had the ark of God

on hand they were assured of victory. Their enemies, the Philistines, were genuinely scared about this, but it only made them more determined to defeat Israel. The same is true for us. We cannot command God's blessing by observing religious rituals and presumption is the father of all foul ups! This is true both individually and corporately. Many churches should rename themselves St Ichabod's because God just ain't there! You can put a building up, place a cross on the top, put a man in a dog collar in the pulpit and do all the right things – and God can still be totally absent. There will be no glory, no presence of God, if there is no genuine revelation, no vision.

The greatest commandment

In Mark chapter 12 we read about an incident where a teacher of the Law asks Jesus, *"Of all the commandments, which is the most important?"* (Mark 12:28, NIV). Jesus answers unequivocally, *"Hear, O Israel, the Lord our God, the Lord is one. Love the Lord your God with all your heart and with all your soul and with all your mind and with all your strength"* (Mark 12:29–30, NIV). What is interesting about Jesus' statement is that it is not one of the Ten Commandments. You would think that Jesus would simply say, "The first one." Instead, Jesus' words echo those of Moses in Deuteronomy 6:5. This was Moses' explanation to the people of Israel of what the Law was all about. It was a summary of the whole Law.

Jesus was saying that the way to keep the whole law is to concentrate on loving Him with all our heart, soul, mind and strength.[1] This principle applies to each commandment. If we want to avoid idolatry then we focus on God. So when God commands us to have no other gods but Him, our response can be a positive one: to concentrate our love and attention on Him. Maybe we would rather go and watch a football match than spend time with God or, in my case, go bowling? That's fine, but we cannot then presume we will enjoy God's presence and blessing in our life. God says that we will find Him when we seek Him with all our heart. God is not a "just turn up" easy person. He wants to be all or nothing to us.

Yet, God is not legalistic. He is a God of grace. Often God blesses us despite our lifestyle, but that is just His sheer goodness towards us and we should not make the mistake of thinking it is His stamp of approval on our lifestyle. But neither should we live under the fear that if we don't put God first, something terrible will happen to us. God is not capricious like that. He doesn't treat us like we treat Him.

I was speaking to a man once whose daughter had finally left home. "Dad," she said, "come round and look at my flat." It was the middle of winter at the time. He walked in and said, "This is nice!" and then proceeded to go around the place turning the thermostats on the radiators up to full. Then he opened all the windows in the flat and turned on every ring on the gas hob. Finally, he asked if he could phone his cousin in Australia. Horrified, his daughter protested, "Dad, what are you doing? You'll bankrupt me!" And he replied, "You've done that to me for the past eighteen years in my house!"

The point is, when the girl was paying the gas bill herself she realized the cost! When God commanded us to have no other gods apart from Him, He did so fully prepared to pay the cost. When we throw our lot in with God He commits Himself to providing for all our needs – everything – now and forever. He promises never to leave us or forsake us. When we are in need He never says to us, "I'm busy today. Try another god!" If we put Him first then He will lavish on us all His love, time, attention and provision. He truly becomes our Jehovah Jireh – the Lord our Provider.

Joshua experienced the same challenges we do today in our pluralistic society. The children of Israel, God's own people, had integrated the gods of their previous and current cultures into the worship of Almighty God. But at the beginning of Joshua's ministry he is commanded by God to be "strong and of good courage". Joshua was instructed to not turn to the left or to the right – in other words to not take the middle ground and compromise. In Joshua chapter 24 we see him confronting the issue of "other gods" with the people:

> " 'Now therefore,' he said, 'put away the foreign gods which are among you, and incline your heart to the Lord God of Israel.' "
>
> (Joshua 24:23)

The people had a choice: to serve "the gods of their fathers" or the one true God. Joshua nailed his colours to the mast:

> "As for me and my house, we will serve the Lord."
>
> (Joshua 24:15)

We must not make excuses for ourselves, blaming our nature, our background or our preferences when the Lord calls them "foreign gods"! Identify those beliefs and desires that are alien to a kingdom lifestyle and deal ruthlessly with them.

Note
1. "The Greatest Commandment" is covered in detail in the last chapter.

You Shall Not Make for Yourself a Carved Image

"You shall not make for yourself a carved image – any likeness of anything that is in heaven above, or that is in the earth beneath, or that is in the water under the earth; you shall not bow down to them nor serve them. For I, the LORD your God, am a jealous God, visiting the iniquity of the fathers upon the children to the third and fourth generations of those who hate Me, but showing mercy to thousands, to those who love Me and keep My commandments."

(Exodus 20:4–6)

One criticism that is constantly levelled at the Ten Commandments and the Bible in general is that they are out of date and out of touch with the real world. "How can these archaic commandments written thousands of years ago to a relatively small group of people be relevant to us now?" sceptics ask. And of all God's laws, this second commandment could seem, on the surface, to be the most outmoded of them all.

The contention of this book, of course, is that the commandments are vitally relevant for us today. And I would argue that this commandment has as much relevance to our modern society as it did when it was given to the children of Israel. As with all of the commandments, we need to look closely at the principle that God was communicating and not get bogged down by the cultural context into which He was speaking at the time.

Having said that, it is clear that throughout history an examination of every great dynasty will reveal an abundance of craven images. What is a craven or carved image? It is a counterfeit, an attempt by man to create an "image" for himself by bypassing God, the true Image Maker. The apostle Paul stood on Mars Hill, overlooking the Greek capital, and surveyed a pantheon of gods, even multiple representations of the same god, because ever since man lost the ability to walk in the cool of the day with His Creator, his need for a substitute has grown ever stronger.

In Genesis 1:26 we read,

> *"Then God said, 'Let Us make man in Our image, according to Our likeness; let them have dominion over the fish of the sea, over the birds of the air, and over the cattle, over all the earth and over every creeping thing that creeps on the earth.' "*

In the beginning man had an image – God's very own in fact! Man was created in the image of God Himself. What did this mean? It meant that man had the ability to do several things that were innate to God's nature: to speak creatively – in other words, to cause things to be brought about by confession, by speaking forth. It also meant that man had an ability to bind and to release and of course the ability to be loved and to love in return.

God also gave man the ability to express his love through the act of praise and worship. Man was made to worship his Creator, his Father. The Westminster Shorter Catechism states that, "Man's chief end is to glorify God, and to enjoy him forever." The greatest perversion of man's gift of worship occurs when, instead of worshipping God, man worships himself or some image that he has manufactured. Man was never designed to be worshipped, but to be a worshipper. We see that Peter and John resisted any form of adulation after they healed a lame man in Acts chapter 3, and again Peter refused to be exalted when he visited the house of Cornelius in Acts chapter 10:

> "As Peter entered the house, Cornelius met him and fell at his feet in reverence. But Peter made him get up. 'Stand up,' he said, 'I am only a man myself.' "   (Acts 10:25–26, NIV)

When we talk about man being made in God's "image", the Hebrew word used in Genesis chapter 1 means "a resemblance" or "a representative figure". Man was made in the "likeness" of God and manifests God-like characteristics in human form. The disciples began to be referred to as "Christians" at Antioch because they *resembled* Christ. It was a term initiated by the non-believing population of Antioch who referred to the disciples literally as "little Christs". It was probably meant in a mocking or derisory way, but eventually believers began to use the term when referring to themselves as a name of honour and not shame (see Acts 26:28; 1 Peter 4:16).

In the beginning Adam was God's "representative" in a world He had created out of chaos. Adam's role was to have dominion over God's creation and to rule it effectively. He was a little version of God with limited powers and God-like duties to perform. Tragically, after man's fall through sin, he corrupted and distotred his own image. This is the first instance where man decided to use a "mask" to try to conceal his true identity. Adam and Eve, covering their nakedness with leaves and hiding in the undergrowth, were terrified of being exposed. Mankind has been using masks to hide behind ever since.

Despite the fall, however, mankind's natural God-consciousness remains. Every person alive knows that there is "something missing" in their life and tries to fill it by a plethora of means. God wants to have a relationship with man that is based on need, but man wants to have a relationship with his "god", whatever it may be, based on greed. Cain and his brother Abel dramatically illustrate the contrast between these opposing philosophies. Cain maintained a self-created façade of spirituality and brought an offering of pride to God. Abel recognized his genuine need of his Creator and brought an offering born out of humility. One offered dead fruit and the other a living sacrifice.

Manmade images

A carved image – whether it be a literal one i.e. a wooden god purchased from a market stall in some pagan culture – or an idol created by the manipulation of the media such as a footballing legend or a pop megastar – is man's attempt to play God, to make his own creation to worship and to give him fulfilment. It is a total reversal of Creation. Isaiah chapter 44 speaks about the absolute folly of such an approach:

"He cuts down cedars for himself,
And takes the cypress and the oak;
He secures it for himself among the trees of the forest.
He plants a pine, and the rain nourishes it.
Then it shall be for a man to burn,
For he will take some of it and warm himself;
Yes, he kindles it and bakes bread;
Indeed he makes a god and worships it;
He makes it a carved image, and falls down to it.
He burns half of it in the fire;
With this half he eats meat;
He roasts a roast, and is satisfied.
He even warms himself and says,
'Ah! I am warm,
I have seen the fire.'
And the rest of it he makes into a god,
His carved image.
He falls down before it and worships it,
Prays to it and says,
'Deliver me, for you are my god!'
They do not know nor understand;
For He has shut their eyes, so that they cannot see,
And their hearts, so that they cannot understand.
And no one considers in his heart,
Nor is there knowledge nor understanding to say,
'I have burned half of it in the fire,
Yes, I have also baked bread on its coals;
I have roasted meat and eaten it;
And shall I make the rest of it an abomination?
Shall I fall down before a block of wood?'
He feeds on ashes;

A deceived heart has turned him aside;
And he cannot deliver his soul,
Nor say, 'Is there not a lie in my right hand?'"

              (Isaiah 44:14–20)

In other words, the Bible says, "How stupid!" The prophet lays open the futility of manmade images. From the same tree a person uses wood to make a fire, warm himself up, cook food, and then with the leftovers he makes an image and falls down to worship it!

Clearly, this is a blatant example and I hear you say, "David, I wouldn't be that silly!" Wouldn't you? The subtlety of idolatry, for that is what it is, means that it is often apparent to others much more than it is to us. Look how easily the children of Israel fell into idolatry as soon as Moses was off the scene. Whilst he was up the mountain conversing with God, the people were busy making a golden calf to worship.

> *"Now when the people saw that Moses delayed coming down from the mountain, the people gathered together to Aaron, and said to him, 'Come, make us gods that shall go before us; for as for this Moses, the man who brought us up out of the land of Egypt, we do not know what has become of him.'"*
>
>   (Exodus 32:1)

How incredibly short-sighted when the Lord had only just displayed His power to the people and executed a mighty deliverance for them to release them from the bondage of Egypt. It was Moses who had led the way during that victory. Now, as soon as his back was turned they were setting up an idol!

Moses, by the way, was not delaying in coming down from the mountain; he was immersed in the presence of Almighty God! Can you ever be delayed by the presence of God? I think not. But the people had no concept of such things. They called for a new image. A golden calf held a greater appeal to them than a sacrificed lamb. Even Aaron, Moses' brother and constant companion throughout his dealings with God, was deceived. Seemingly without batting an eyelid, his response to the people was,

> " 'Break off the golden earrings which are in the ears of your wives, your sons, and your daughters, and bring them to me.' So all the people broke off the golden earrings which were in their ears, and brought them to Aaron. And he received the gold from their hand, and he fashioned it with an engraving tool, and made a moulded calf." (Exodus 32:2–4)

How did that happen? How was Aaron so readily sucked into their deception? He must have lost the plot long before this moment of testing. In modern terms the children of Israel still came to church, still tithed, but had decided to become ultra-seeker-friendly with a new image and logo!

Moses, who was in tune with God, heard the Lord speak to him saying,

> "Go, get down! For your people whom you brought out of the land of Egypt have corrupted themselves. They have turned aside quickly out of the way which I commanded them. They have made themselves a moulded calf, and worshipped it and sacrificed to it, and said, 'This is your god, O Israel, that brought you out of the land of Egypt!' " (Exodus 32:7–8)

Young Joshua who accompanied Moses up the mountain thought the great noise he could hear in the distance was the sound of the people in victory (verse 17) – but he was wrong. It was the sound of disaster! When Moses confronted his brother Aaron and asked him what he had done, his excuse was lame to say the least:

> *"So they gave it* [the gold] *to me, and I cast it into the fire, and this calf came out."*   (Exodus 32:24)

Whenever sin is exposed the excuses say it all!

Today, just as in Moses' day, consumerism has joined forces with the demands of the populous to create images that try to pacify man's inner need to give out worship and adoration. The late 50s and 60s saw the first "pop idols" created. Not the modern TV show, but the originals! Fans could worship a representation of their idol carved out of plastic and running at 45rpm. Bands such as The Beatles became icons as thousands of hysterically screaming teenagers poured adulation upon them whenever they appeared on stage or in public. Countless thousands of pounds were spent in the pursuit of collecting a vast array of memorabilia so that followers could create their own little shrine at home in honour of their heroes! Elvis, the icon with greatest longevity of any, has sold more albums since his death than in his lifetime.

The trap of personal image mania

Recently a piece of research was carried out that examined society's view of success as portrayed in American literature over the last two centuries. First the first 150 of the last 200 years "success" in life was largely defined by one's possession of high moral integrity and a hard work ethic. In the last 50 years the focus of success has become much more about the things we own than the quality of our character. Success, in modern society, is defined by how we win friends and influence people, by the car we drive, the clothes we wear, the place where we live, and our physical attributes. The first 150 years was about character and the last 50 years has been about "additives". Very superficial. Remember the old adage: It's not what you own, it's what owns you.

I am blessed to pastor a large, blessed and thriving church, but in many circles I am viewed with suspicion. Some see me as if I were the slick CEO of a burgeoning mega-church. If you were to ask me, I would honestly answer you: Yes, we do run multiple services on a Sunday and we do it professionally – we have to be efficient; yes, I write books (like this one!) and I also have lots of CDs and DVDs of my teaching – it is the best way to reach as many people as possible with the message of Jesus Christ; yes, I travel and speak at conferences on big platforms – but I do so only as the Holy Spirit prompts me, not because I need to do it to bolster my self-worth.

But if you were to ask me, am I creating a one-man ministry, a church that revolves around me, the answer is categorically, no! We must avoid the "one-man-ministry" model of church. All some people are doing is creating a virtual brand for themselves – the pastor and his wife wearing designer clothing, living in the best part of town, with their pictures prominently displayed on every bit of promotional material that comes out of the church. All this achieves is to help people slip into the very trap of idolatry we are trying to avoid as the leaders are put on a pedestal and revered. The need to create such "images" for ourselves has no better motive than the one that caused Aaron to fashion the golden calf. Let's not fall into the trap of thinking our faith is about getting what we want out of our relationship with God. It is all about Calvary, not consumerism.

A jealous God

The latter half of the second commandment tells us the reason why God abhors the sin of idolatry and the creation of man-made images to worship.

> *"For I, the* LORD *your God, am a jealous God, visiting the iniquity of the fathers upon the children to the third and fourth generations of those who hate Me, but showing mercy to thousands, to those who love Me and keep My commandments."*
> (Exodus 20:5–6)

Most people would consider jealousy a sin and so find it hard to fathom that God is jealous, but it should really be interpreted as "zealous". God is passionate about His people and passionate about their welfare. He is totally enthusiastic in His love and devotion to His children, His creation who manifest His image. For that reason He is jealous for us, knowing that a devotion to Him will reap the best rewards for our lives.

Because idolatry is such a serious sin – denying the very image of God and replacing it with something abominable – it has dire consequences. However, I want to clear up some erroneous teaching that has become common recently in some Charismatic circles. People who have suffered from problems in their life have been told, "Ah, it's because you have been cursed to the fourth generation and so you need deliverance." I want to point out that God is not capable of doing what these people are suggesting has happened! It is not in God's nature to demonise someone as a punishment for their sin – let alone their ancestor's sin. First of all, this scripture refers to the successive generations of "... *those who hate Me* [God]". There are no Christians (and not many non-Christians) who actively hate God! Secondly, when God talks about someone being under a curse it is not because He has decided to inflict a curse upon them; it happens as a consequence of God withdrawing His blessing from that person because they have turned their back on Him.

When God withdraws His blessing from a person they are immediately "limited". In other words, they could own everything they desire in life, but still be unhappy and unfulfilled. God says those who hate Him will have a limitation on them that will last up to four generations. I'm sure most of us know people who seem to have such limitations upon them. It doesn't matter how much money they get, they are always broke. They are never out of debt. They are limited.

Conversely, you see people who honour God prospering though they have very little. Many of us will also know people who, though they don't earn very much, still manage to live in a nice house, always have food on the table and manage to go away on holidays. Why? Because a spiritual principle is at work – it is the blessing of God brought about by obedience to Him. When you are living under a curse (the absence of God's blessing) you see a contrary spiritual principle at work. The more you earn the more you spend just to keep your head above water. But all this is nothing to do with the demonic. For someone oppressed by demons totally different spiritual principles are at work. So please don't use the fourth generational curse as a proof text for deliverance ministry!

Another aspect of this principle is sheer common sense if you think about it. God says that if you hate Him it will affect your children and their children and so on. If a man runs his house in an ungodly, God-hating way, then of course it will affect his children! Remember the chapter on honouring your father and mother? We are a product of our family, whether we like it or not! We are two-thirds our parents, genetically speaking.

Yet, God's blessing always outweighs any possible curse. The scripture says that God shows mercy to thousands – multiple generations – of those who love Him and keep His commandments. God's mercy and grace is far greater than His judgement. By hating God you lose His blessing, but by loving God you instinctively keep His commandments, because keeping the commandments are a visible, external sign of an invisible, inwardly transformed heart, and you are blessed.

Keep God at the centre of your thoughts. Let not a lifeless icon in the likeness of anything become a substitute deity in your life – whether it is a lifestyle, image consciousness, money, clothes, cars, or whatever. If they cannot speak or hear or see, how can they offer you anything?

You Shall Not Take the Name of the Lord Your God in Vain

"You shall not take the name of the Lord your God in vain,
for the Lord will not hold him guiltless
who takes His name in vain."
(Exodus 20:7)

In Exodus 20:7 God gives His people a short, yet vital command:

> *"You shall not take the name of the Lord your God in vain, for the Lord will not hold him guiltless who takes His name in vain."*

There are three important things to note about this verse:

1. It speaks about the name of the Lord
2. It speaks about vain application
3. It speaks about guilt

We have to remember that the laws of God were given twice. The first time they were unveiled they gave a startling revelation of who God was and what His character was like. Until then, God had no relationship with the people of Israel on a personal, one-to-one basis. Relationship with God was achieved only through divinely appointed prophets, priests and kings. No ordinary person could commune with God directly, so the average person knew little about Him and what He was like.

The first issue of the Ten Commandments changed this. God was willing to make Himself vulnerable to the people and reveal more about Himself. He revealed that He was a God committed to love, single-minded and single-hearted. The Commandments also showed what God was *not* like: He was not covetous or adulterous. The whole point of the first unveiling of the Commandments was to reveal God's character as a role model for the people to follow; to inspire them with His beauty, holiness and majesty. Inspiration engages perspiration.

Lamentably, while Moses was still on the mountain speaking with God, having received the Commandments, the people of Israel fell into gross idolatry. They managed to coerce Moses' brother Aaron into adding and abetting them, and they created for themselves a golden calf to worship. God interrupted his dialogue with Moses to tell him, "Go down because your people have defiled themselves."

When Moses reached the camp he smashed the God-given Commandments in anger because of the sin of the people. In essence he declared, "God has been loving and vulnerable enough to show you His heart, but you have polluted yourself. You don't deserve to see and understand the character of God." So Moses smashed the stone tablets.

Moses went back to God after this incident and discussed the matter once again. God, who does not change, had not changed

His mind about the Commandments and they were re-written, but this time their emphasis (and their significance to Israel) had changed. Rather than providing inspiration for His people, the Commandments now revealed how impossible it was for them to keep God's law and aspire to be like Him in His character. This produced guilt. Man is now judged because he does not keep the Commandments, as this particular command points out: "Take not the Lord's name in vain or *you will be found guilty*."

Using God's name in vain

God's law is God's law and the Bible is explicit about that. There is no allowance for mitigating circumstances, no opportunity to present circumstantial evidence or to have people speak on your behalf. It's quite simple: anybody who uses the Lord God's name in vain will be found guilty.

But first, we must be clear about what "taking the Lord's name in vain" actually means. It does not mean, as many people imagine, saying, "Oh God!" or misusing the name of Jesus by substituting it as a swear word. To misuse God's name in this way is certainly blasphemous, but it is not what this commandment is addressing. Instead, God is speaking about man's *attitude* towards His name.

The word "vain" in Hebrew in the context of this verse means "desolating" or "to bring into desolation". In other words, that which was once prosperous and productive is robbed of its potency. When something is desolate it is devoid of life, devoid of action. The Hebrew word translated vain also means "to destroy" and another facet of its meaning is "guile" or "deception" – to have another agenda, to use cunning, or to have a purpose for something other than that which is appropriate.

Deception occurs when we give the impression of something that isn't true – another word for lying! In modern usage we have coined the phrase, "He/she is so vain" and take it to mean when a person looks in the mirror thinking they are gorgeous when in fact they are not. Vanity can cause a person to have a personal "blind spot" where certain aspects of their life are concerned. An example that springs to mind is the many unsuccessful auditionees of reality shows the *X Factor* and *American Idol* – people who, mostly through vanity, are under the false impression that they are talented singers! Some claim to be the next great undiscovered talent of their nation, yet they are appalling!

Hebrew is a rich language and a single word can express many concepts, rather than a single meaning. The word "vain" can also "mean empty, worthless, futile and shallow". Paul spoke about the concept of vanity when he wrote, "Even though I speak with the language of angels and of men, if I speak in those tongues yet have not love, I'm empty." In other words, where there is vanity there is a lack of substance and therefore what is born of vanity has no intrinsic value.

Vanity occurs where there is an absence of honour. Simply put, taking God's name in vain means we do not honour His name as we should, and this can outwork itself in a number of ways. For instance, vanity is acting as if we have authority in God's name, yet living a lifestyle that contradicts that. A perfect example of this is found in Acts 19:13–16. The apostle Paul, whose ministry was characterised by the power of God, was seeing amazing things happen. People would bring hand-kerchiefs to him to pray over, take them back to their ailing relatives and they would be healed – without Paul even being present. However, some people tried to replicate this ministry of power, taking Jesus' name in vain, with disastrous results.

> *"Then some of the itinerant Jewish exorcists took it upon themselves to call the name of the Lord Jesus over those who had evil spirits, saying, 'We exorcise you by the Jesus whom Paul preaches.' Also there were seven sons of Sceva, a Jewish chief priest, who did so. And the evil spirit answered and said, 'Jesus I know, and Paul I know; but who are you?' Then the man in whom the evil spirit was leaped on them, overpowered them, and prevailed against them, so that they fled out of that house naked and wounded."* (Acts 19:13–16)

People came to realize that the name of Jesus had great potency and power; they saw the results of the apostles' ministry in His name, and they must have been startled when they realized that demons knew the name of Jesus. This verse indicates that two groups of people began using Jesus' name in vain. First, there were people referred to as "exorcists" – those who dabbled in the spirit world and tried to cast demons out of people. There is a similar account to the one above recounted in Acts chapter 9 where Peter encounters a character called "Simon the sorcerer" who, having witnessed the power of God in action, tried to "buy" the gifts of the Spirit for himself.

Here, in Acts 19, we see the seven sons of a Jewish chief priest falling into error as they try, without any relationship with the Living God, to invoke the name of Jesus to cast out demons. This second group of people actually had an impressive religious heritage. What this highlights to me is that you can be a spiritualist/exorcist – someone who is clearly not walking with God – or you can come from a well-respected religious family, the son/daughter of a senior minister, and still not know the power of God through relationship with Him in your own life. That is why it is so essential, especially where kids are brought up in a Christian home, for every person to cultivate their individual relationship with God through Jesus. You cannot live on borrowed faith!

Both groups of people knew that there was, without doubt, power in the name of Jesus. The Bible says that it is the name that is above every other name and that at the name of Jesus *"every knee shall bow and every tongue confess that Jesus Christ is Lord."* There is a uniqueness in the name of Jesus. His name is Emmanuel meaning "God with us". He is "the Lord" because He is Jehovah Himself as Hebrews 1:3 tells us. And He is also the Christ – the anointed One. In Scripture, many names are used to describe God and reveal a different facet of His character – and every one of those names has power.

Yet, these men did not truly know the owner of "the name" or the power of His name. This is apparent in this verse not just because of the reaction of the demons, but because the men use the phrase "by the Jesus whom Paul preaches". Is the name of Jesus powerful in your life or somebody else's? I want people to know God for themselves and to be able to declare, "In the name of Jesus whom I serve..." It would be pointless for a member of our congregation to pray, "In the name of the God who answers Pastor Dave..."! We need to know the power of God firsthand in our own lives.

In recent times I have had the privilege of speaking and ministering to a number of leading Anglicans. The Archbishop of York is a good friend of mine. But those relationships will not give me any more spiritual authority than I have already. They may open doors for me in the Anglican church, but they open nothing in heaven! If I was asked to go and preach before the Pope at the Vatican and received his blessing, that still wouldn't get me anywhere because he is just a man. Spiritual authority is bestowed on an individual only by God and comes out of that person's relationship with Him. The demonic forces recognize authentic power and can immediately identify those who are anointed by God. The demons responded immediately to the sons of Sceva's attempts at deliverance by calling out, "Paul we know, whom you talk about and Jesus we know, but who are you?"

The demons' response confirms two things for us:

1. These men were taking the name of God in vain – they did not know the authority of His name.
2. But, secondly and interestingly, the demons did not know who those people were. This contradicts the teaching of some deliverance ministries who maintain that (a) the majority of people are demonised, and (b) that the demonic forces have complete knowledge of who every person is.

This scripture shows us plainly that these demons hadn't got a clue who these people were. There is some weird demonology being taught in the Church today that is unhelpful and misleading. Our focus and attention in our spiritual warfare should be centred on Jesus, not on the demonic. We give the devil and his forces more credibility than they deserve; we attribute more authority to them than they actually have. Every person does not have a demon – there aren't that many to go around! Demons cannot reproduce themselves and yet the human population of the world continues to grow. To say that everyone is afflicted by demonic forces defies logic!

However, when man does come into contact with demons, they understand whether a person is a vain user of God's name or the genuine article. Demons know when a person is using Jesus' name without the power of relationship to back up their words. They also know when a person is using His name with guile and deceit – in other words, to build a ministry for themselves; to improve their own credibility.

As a result, the demons that the sons of Sceva confronted refuse to budge. If these men had possessed true spiritual power the demons would have fled. Similarly, just because we pray in the name of Jesus, it doesn't mean that the sick will be healed; it doesn't mean that demons will flee; it doesn't mean that people will be born again. Those things only happen where the anointing of God is present.

Solomon, in a time of great distress, said in Ecclesiastes 1:2, *"Vanity of vanities, all is vanity."* In other words, "All is emptiness, all is deceit." The wisest man of earth mentioned the word thirty-seven times throughout this book. By contrast, the apostle Paul was ever vigilant that his ministry did not become futile and useless. He wanted to be a productive worker in the kingdom of God. "Oh that my preaching was not in vain amongst you!" he said. He did not want to be empty and deceitful, but desired to move in the truth and power of the Holy Spirit. Paul knew and understood this simple fact which we all need to grasp: *When we come in vanity before God, we neutralise His power in our lives.*

This is the very reason God gave this commandment. It wasn't a reprimand – a slap around the head. It is not God saying, "Don't you dare speak about me like that!" Rather,

God wants to spare us from a futile, empty existence that lacks His power and presence. He wants us to experience the real thing, not some pale, insipid imitation.

Taking on the name of God

The greatest thing God can bestow upon us is to be associated with His name; to be identified as "one who belongs to Him". If we abuse that privilege by acting in vanity, then we neutralise the power of His name. If we honour God's name and act out of our relationship with Him, we will know His power working in and through us.

Let's think a bit further about "what's in a name?" Our name is our title, our label, the designation by which we are known and distinguishable from others. Remember at school when the teacher would call out your name whilst taking the register? We each have a name so that we can be identified. Even identical twins do not have the same name. Though it may be hard to tell which is which by their physical features, their unique names separate them. Our name is a distinguishing factor.

How you conduct yourself determines other people's opinion of you and, importantly, it affects how people view others who share the same name as you. Think about that for a moment. Isn't it true that if you had a really bad experience with a person called Fred, every time you meet another Fred you are reminded of it? You may even become wary of "Freds" altogether! When I was at school I was bullied terribly by a girl named Susan. It's awful for any person to be bullied, but for a boy to be bullied by a girl is particularly humiliating. There were two reasons why Susan managed to bully me.

One, because at the time I was exceptionally wimpish, and two, because she looked like she had graduated from a school of Russian weightlifters! Her name should have been Olga! I could understand why Johnny Cash wrote a song called, "A boy named Sue". She used to slap me and a number of the younger kids around terribly. As a result, it took me many years, even as a Christian, to relate well to anyone called Susan. In the end I said to God, "Lord, there are some lovely women called Sue, but unless you help me and heal me from that hurt I will always look at them with a wrong perspective." Needless to say, God took that past hurt away from me.

If you are in any doubt about the power names hold then think about this: how much do we identify with what names mean to us when we name our children? Often people will name their kids after people who have been their heroes, or after someone who has meant a great deal to them. Conversely, people will say things like, "We're not calling her that – that was your great aunt's name and you know what she was like!" or, "It's a nice name, but it has bad connotations in our family." Names speak of a person's character. That's why no one tends to name their child "Adolf"!

In African culture people's names take on a much greater significance than in the West. People are often named according to the circumstances surrounding their birth and will have unusual names meaning things like, "fine weather" or "born on a Monday". Their names say something about them. In the West we tend to choose names just because we like the sound of them and the meaning is very much a secondary issue, if it is thought about at all.

I'm sure my parents didn't pick the name David for me because of its meaning; they didn't have a spiritual dimension to their lives in those days. But sometimes God allows an "accident" to become a truth. At a time when I hated myself and wished I had never been born, someone came to me and said, "What a lovely name David is. It means 'You'll be loved'." When I didn't love myself God had decided that my name would declare something different; it would carry the seed of my future.

A name can also designate the relationship that exists between two entities, and this is especially true of God and His people. Certain names immediately evoke a reaction from us because they are the names of our loved ones. Specific names are important to us because they define the relationships that surround our life. Recently I married a lovely young couple called Chris and Hannah. If I mention the name "Chris" to Hannah she won't shudder and say, "Don't mention that name!", because it's the name of the man she has married! The name "Chris" immediately evokes feelings of warmth and fondness for her.

Now we understand the importance of a name, how much more should we honour and protect the name of God? The name of Jesus? His name is precious, strong and powerful. There is no other name to be compared to His name. The Bible says it is the *only name* in all heaven and earth by which man can be saved. If you misuse that name, then you are in big trouble.

Another of the Commandments deals with the important issue of bearing false witness towards fellow human beings, but the essence of this commandment is to do with bearing false witness towards God – misrepresenting Him. This aspect of the commandment was played out in the life of Job. Job was a man who was protected by God and lived in pure prosperity. His relationship with God was one of covenant and mutual esteem.

Job's understanding of the magnitude of God, His name and His authority, was secure. So it was he whom God chose to champion the cause of righteousness and honour His name. The devil's attack on Job was an attempt to get him, above all, to take God's name in vain.

When the devil said, "I can't find anybody to test" God said, "Have you thought of Job, my servant?" Just think about that for a moment. Imagine being nominated by Almighty God to represent His name. The Lord said about Job, "He's blameless and upright, fears God and shuns evil." What awesome credentials God gave him.

The devil tried to link Job's faithfulness to God with patronage. In other words, he contested that Job only honoured God because God was blessing him. This was the devil's challenge: "The only reason Job doesn't lie about you, the only reason he doesn't fall out with you and is not devious with you, is because you bless him. If you stop doing that he'll abuse your name!" In actual fact, this incident had little to do with Job. It was the name of the Lord that was on trial. But God insisted, *"Still he holds fast to his integrity, although you incited Me against him, to destroy him without cause"* (Job 2:3).

A person who does not abuse the name of the Lord is a person of integrity and faithfulness who shuns evil according to God. Job was such a person, but he was severely tested, even by those closest to him. Job's wife challenged the basis of his relationship with God and tried to get him to take God's name in vain: "Do you still hold fast to your integrity? Curse God and die!"

Here is another important principle for us to take on board: take the Lord's name in vain and you will die – not physically, but certainly spiritually and emotionally. We die relationally when we begin to abuse the name of God. In whatever area of life we decide to dishonour His name, that area becomes inaccessible to Him. We effectively block His blessing in that area and the joy of the Lord begins to leave us. We neutralise the effect of His lordship, His name, in that area of our life.

If you are lacking joy in your life at present, it is possible that you have neutralised the name of the Lord in an area of your life. If you lack the strength to overcome, if you go from sickness to sickness, if you are constantly tired and feeling persecuted, if your business is failing ... it is likely that you have neutralised the power of God in your life because you have lived in His name with vanity, falsehood and guile. You may not be admitting the truth about the depth of your relationship with God. Whenever we misrepresent the name of the Lord by claiming His name and yet living a life unworthy of His name we restrict His ability to move in our life.

Jesus Himself had His ministry restricted by a lack of honour for His name. Jesus was not able to do many miracles in His home town because, as He put it, *"A prophet is not without honour except in his own country and in his own house"* (Matthew 13:57).

Looking back at the two verses preceding this statement we can see the attitude that the locals held towards Jesus:

> *"Is this not the carpenter's son? Is not His mother called Mary? And His brothers James, Joses, Simon, and Judas? And His sisters, are they not all with us? Where then did this Man get all these things?"*   (Matthew 13:55–56)

Because the people had downgraded His name it was imposs-ible for Jesus to do many miracles there. If you don't believe that the name of Jesus has the power to break sin, sickness and fear, well, there is no other name on offer! No other name has the power to change lives and eternal destines except Jesus. Buddha hasn't done it, Muhammad hasn't done it, Confucius hasn't done it. There is no Plan B for mankind – only Jesus!

Name dropping

Everyone tends to name drop from time to time. It's a natural tendency we all have. But do we drop the name of Jesus as much as we should? Have you ever been a bit embarrassed or ashamed to speak out the name of Jesus in certain circles? In a business meeting? On an aeroplane? At the supermarket? At school? Do you stand up for God's name? Or is it easier to say, "I go to church" than "I'm a Christian and I believe in Jesus"? Are we too politically correct, afraid of offending others with our faith?

I hate political correctness and so does my wife Molly! When someone asks her, "What's you partner's name?" she typically responds, "I haven't got one." Then if the person says, "Oh, are you single?" she will say, "No, I've got a husband – one of those things that nobody mentions these days!" In the world of political correctness kids don't have fathers, they have "guardians" in case the man who is living at home isn't their biological father. It's craziness! We need to stand up for the names we own, the names we are in relationship with, and say it like it is. This is my son, my daughter, my wife, my husband; this is my church; I belong to Jesus ... we need to own up to these names!

Job confessed the name of the Lord and he didn't use any vain words. In Job 1:20–22 we read that,

"Job arose, tore his robe, and shaved his head; and he fell to the ground and worshipped. And he said:

> *'Naked I came from my mother's womb,*
> *And naked shall I return there.*
> *The LORD gave, and the LORD has taken away;*
> *Blessed be the name of the LORD.'*

In all this Job did not sin nor charge God with wrong."

The New Living Translation says, *"Job did not sin by blaming God"* and the Amplified Bible renders this verse, *"Job sinned not nor charged God foolishly."* In the NIV it says, *"Job did not sin by charging God with wrongdoing."* Had Job done any of these things he would have removed himself from the full provision of the Lord's protection. As Proverbs 18:10 says, *"The name of the LORD is a strong tower; the righteous run to it and are safe."*

The Amplified Bible adds an enlightening word into the last part of that verse and uses the phrase, "consistently righteous". Here is another key for us: we need to be consistently righteous in order to receive the full benefit of God's power in our lives. If you have been praying and no answer has come it is worth taking a personal inventory to see if there is any area in your life in which you have been compromising. This may be the key to unlocking your problem. Many people have an attitude that says, "I want God to do something for me so I'd better be righteous today." Because they need God to move on their behalf they decide that today they will not watch any dubious TV programmes, have too much to drink, lie or flirt, then maybe God will do a miracle for them. But tomorrow they will go back to doing the same things they did before. No! The consistently righteous have a strong tower in the name of Jesus, not the manipulative who seek God when it suits them or when there is a crisis!

In Acts 5, right at the beginning of the establishment of the Church, a man and his wife died for taking the Lord's name in vain. Acts 5:3 says, *"Peter said, 'Ananias, why has Satan filled your heart to lie to the Holy Spirit and keep back part of the price of the land for yourself?'"* In the Amplified version verse 9 says that this couple, *"... agreed and conspired together to try to deceive the Spirit of the Lord."*

Ananias and Sapphira both found themselves guilty of taking the Lord's name in vain. They omitted to realize that God is omniscient; He knows everything! They were being two-faced – giving the outward appearance of being obedient to God when actually they were driven by self-will and consumed with self-desire.

Many a person falls into a similar trap today – though the consequences of our actions are not so immediate and final as they were for Ananias and Sapphira. God's name is often quoted to support numerous whims and fancies. Many Evangelical, Pentecostal and Charismatic Christians preface every remark they make with, "God told me..." or "God led me...". They say, "I felt led to do this..." As Gerald Coates once said, " A lot of Christians suffer from 'felt led poisoning'"! Most would die of fright if they truly heard the voice of God addressing them!

I caution the members of our church to be very careful before attributing the name of God to something. I have often had conversations with people that went along the lines of, "Pastor Dave, the Lord is telling me to do this ... will you support me in it?" Sometimes I have to respond, "That's not God who's spoken to you." "Why is it not God?" the person replies, offended. "Because God never contradicts His Word and what you're saying He's telling you to do is not in His Word. You're taking His name in vain."

Too many people use God's name to endorse their decision to leave their church, join another church, leave ministries etc. They would be much more honest if they admitted, "I'm really cheesed off with church at the moment, and if I'm honest I probably need to take a good look at my attitude and figure out why." Over the years I have heard every excuse in the book for people leaving churches: "God told me I was only here for a season" is one of the most popular. More often than not, the real reason for their departure is either that somebody or something has offended them and they can't get over it, or they wanted to do something (lead worship, become a full-time member of staff, start a ministry) and failed to get the backing of the leadership team. They say, "God has told me it's time to move on", but they are actually being two-faced – making it look as though the Lord is actively leading them when in reality they are deeply offended and won't admit the truth.

We must stop using God's name to justify our actions. It's just as bad as deciding what we want God to say to us and then flicking through the Bible until we find a scripture that supports what we want to hear. Pointless! And dangerous too. As a leader it is very hard to disagree with someone who says, "God told me ... " if what they are proposing sounds legitimate. The danger is that they then go off and do it, without actually having heard the voice of God, and the whole endeavour collapses around them like a house of cards. That is what happens when you "go" but are not "sent".

The time is long overdue for many Christians to take an inventory of their lives and examine where they may be taking the Lord's name in vain. So many people do it, almost without realizing, to give themselves spiritual credence, but it's not truthful and it is certainly vanity. Let's be careful about what we say God has told us to do, because we all make mistakes and I'm sure that you, like me, don't want to dishonour the name of the Lord. Remember, this commandment is not a slap on the wrist, but an exhortation to preserve the honour of God's name so that we can live under the full provision of His blessing and protection. Don't neutralise the name of the Lord. Instead, recognize its matchless worth and live to uphold it.

What does the name of Jesus do for us?

It provides, protects and purifies us. It is worthy to be praised. When we live in the safety of His name He cradles us in His arms, caresses our weary souls; He celebrates our victories and consoles us when things are tough.

The name of Jesus bestows righteousness on us and corrects our sin; it counsels us, commands blessing on our life, conceals us in the rock of His salvation, confesses us before the Father.

Jesus is the Lord of our lives and the Christ of every crisis! That's who He is. Let's not take His name in vain.

Remember the Sabbath Day, to Keep it Holy

"Remember the Sabbath day, to keep it holy.
Six days you shall labour and do all your work,
but the seventh day is the Sabbath of the LORD your God.
In it you shall do no work: you, nor your son, nor your daughter,
nor your male servant, nor your female servant, nor your cattle,
nor your stranger who is within your gates.
For in six days the LORD made the heavens and the earth,
the sea, and all that is in them, and rested the seventh day.
Therefore the LORD blessed the Sabbath day and hallowed it."
(Exodus 20:8–11)

In this fourth commandment God instructs His people regarding the pattern their working life should follow: six days of work followed by a day of rest. The word "sabbath" itself simply means "rest". (Note that it does not mean "stay in bed until lunchtime" for those who like to lie in on a Sunday!)

This commandment is very detailed compared to others. God points out that we should not work on the seventh day, nor our children, nor people who are staying with us etc. The

law is very specific here chiefly because the people at that time
did not have the benefit of the guidance of the Holy Spirit. The
law had to be definite and cover every base. People had a
limited understanding of God's ways at that time and so this
kind of precision was necessary. The law also had to be very
strict so that people would take it seriously. In Exodus 31:15–17
we read that there was a severe punishment for violating the
Sabbath:

> *"Work shall be done for six days, but the seventh is the Sabbath
> of rest, holy to the LORD. Whoever does any work on the Sabbath
> day, he shall surely be put to death. Therefore the children of
> Israel shall keep the Sabbath, to observe the Sabbath throughout
> their generations as a perpetual covenant. It is a sign between
> Me and the children of Israel forever; for in six days the LORD
> made the heavens and the earth, and on the seventh day He
> rested and was refreshed."*

God instructed His people that one day per week should be set
aside for "rest and refreshment" and He called it a "perpetual
covenant". In other words this was something that would
never be altered. The principles of God do not change or
suddenly become irrelevant because society changes its work
ethic. Just because Sunday trading has gradually crept more and
more into our culture does not mean the importance of the
Lord's day has diminished for Christians!

It's interesting that God took time out to rest and be
refreshed after completing creation. God does not grow weary
as man grows weary and He never sleeps, so clearly God didn't
need a day off because He was tired! Why did He do it? He set
aside a day of rest as part of the creational process because He

wanted to model for us a pattern of life that included time for reflection and restoration. In His foreknowledge He knew that such a cycle of work–rest would enable man to function at his best. Man needs to engage in work and also have time for recreation (look at the word, literally "re-creation") – a time when we become lost in God's presence, put all other concerns aside for a time, and have our strength restored.

It was by following such a pattern of work and rest that Jesus was able to say, "I do what I see My Father doing and I speak what I hear Him saying." Though He was constantly in demand and busy by any standards, Jesus was scrupulous to protect His time along with His Father. Jesus had a balanced programme of ministry work and rest–recreation time.

God's commandment to His people extended even to gathering food to eat on the Sabbath. Exodus chapter 16 speaks about their journey through the wilderness and how God provided food for them supernaturally. Manna fell from the sky and appeared on the ground each day for the people to go out and collect, but no manna appeared on the Sabbath. Instead, they were instructed to gather up a two-day supply prior to the Sabbath.

> " 'Six days you shall gather it, but on the seventh day, the Sabbath, there will be none ... For the LORD has given you the Sabbath; therefore He gives you on the sixth day bread for two days. Let every man remain in his place; let no man go out of his place on the seventh day.' So the people rested on the seventh day."   (Exodus 16:26, 29–30)

Normally, if the people tried to store manna until the next day it quickly went off and began to smell. The manna that they

collected on the day before the Sabbath, however, did not go off
so quickly – it stayed fresh! So God's people had absolutely no
excuse to break His commandment regarding the Sabbath,
because God provided for their needs. His intention was that
they should rest physically, emotionally and even "financially"
in the sense of not needing to work to get food.

Even non-Christians have understood and taken on board
similar principles over the years. Many employers still pay their
workers "double-time" for working on a Sunday. It is almost as
if they know they are violating a "special" day and so some
extra reward is appropriate. But this misses the point of God's
appointed day of rest. It should have nothing to do with money
and everything to do with spending time with God. I've even
heard people say, "I don't normally work Sundays, Pastor
Dave, but with Christmas coming up, I'll get double time..."
My answer is, "It's always better to trust God to provide for
your needs. You don't need to turn to man-made solutions."

Before anyone comes under condemnation or gets upset
with me, let me be clear about this. There is a big difference
between having a job where you *have* to work on a Sunday
(nurses and doctors for instance) and one where you *choose* to
work on a Sunday. I am not into legalism! But this commandment does speak directly to two kinds of people: those who
don't respect the Lord's day because they are not truly trusting
God for their provision, and those who don't do it because they
think they have no need for rest and refreshment.

I believe both views are serious oversights. The Sabbath is a
day to prove God's creative power by providing for our needs
in six days and His restorative power by replenishing our
energy through resting in His presence. By working seven days
a week, not only will we exhaust ourselves because it is

unsustainable, but we rob God of the pleasure of supplying our needs.

God blessed and sanctified the seventh day and set it apart. It is not and was never intended to be a restriction upon us. Rather it was intended to be a delight. Our flawed human interpretation of God's law always tends to squeeze the life out of His commands and enact them in a legalistic manner. We turn what should be a delight into a punishment! Sunday should be a delightful day to us.

I was brought up as a strict evangelical and Sunday was probably my worst day of the week! Our interpretation of God's law meant that you weren't allowed cook on a Sunday. This meant the food had to be cooked on a Saturday and warmed up. Even then you had to heat it over a very low flame for a long time, because if you heated it over a high flame you would be cooking! Neither could you cut your lawn or wash your car.

I am not mocking those who wish to observe God's law carefully, but when we lose sight of the principles His law is teaching us and begin to interpret them to the best of our human understanding the results are, at best, devilish! We become bound by legalism and the power of the original principle is lost!

Ludicrous things happened when we were kids like being prevented from going to the park to play because "church" effectively lasted all day. Even though I hated school, I used to long for Monday to come around! In Sunday school all our teachers had "Lord's Day Observance Society" badges and the idea was that if you told on one of your friends for buying sweets on a Sunday you got a badge! We practically belonged to the school of Pharisees and Sadducees! The teacher would ask us, "Has anyone bought anything today?" Someone's hand would shoot up: "Excuse me miss, Johnny bought some sherbet on the way here!" Then the teacher would scold the sherbet offender and give the other kid a badge! But after Sunday school, having turned your friend in, you would have some of his sherbet and give him your badge, so the whole thing was a farce!

No wonder that for years I didn't understand the Sabbath, what it really meant, and the depth of its meaning! But eventually I had a revelation of the power of this command-ment and it became a principle I kept all through my business career. I would have rather gone hungry than work on the Lord's day. I even turned down business and lost lucrative contracts for refusing to work on a Sunday. I once lost a personal commission of £25,000 because I refused to go and sign a footballer to a particular club on a Sunday. I said to my employers, "Look, you can have me for six days of the week, but you're not having my Sunday!" Eventually people learned not to bother asking me to work on a Sunday and I believe God honoured me for this. Eventually I began to spend more time pastoring the church and only worked part time. By the time I left business to work full time in ministry I worked just three days a week but earned more in one week than most of my contemporaries earned in a month. God was true to His Word and blessed me with abundantly enough for me to not need to work on a Sunday.

Isaiah 58:13 in the NLT says this:

> "Keep the Sabbath day holy. Don't pursue your own interests on that day, but enjoy the Sabbath and speak of it with delight as the Lord's holy day. Honour the Sabbath in everything you do on that day, and don't follow your own desires or talk idly."

Rather than being restrictive, obeying the Sabbath opens up a prosperity that comes into effect so that all your other days are blessed. The Living Bible version says, *"Enjoy the day and don't go looking for business."*

But there is a startling verse in Isaiah 1:12 that says,

> *"When you come to worship me, who asked you to parade through my courts with all your ceremony?"*   (NLT)

We should realize that God is not interested in us keeping the Sabbath legalistically. The Sabbath is only effective if we recognize what the day is for. Observing it out of a sense of legalistic duty brings no joy to God. In fact, as this verse underlines, He would not even recognize it as worship! Legalism always misses the point. Observing the Sabbath has to do with what happens inside you! It is the time when we meet with the Lord of the Sabbath.

The Pharisees confronted Jesus about infringing the Sabbath in an incident recorded in Matthew chapter 12. Of course, the Pharisees also missed the point of the Sabbath:

> *"At that time Jesus went through the grainfields on the Sabbath. And His disciples were hungry, and began to pluck heads of grain and to eat. And when the Pharisees saw it, they said to Him, 'Look, Your disciples are doing what is not lawful to do on the Sabbath!'*
>
> *But He said to them, 'Have you not read what David did when he was hungry, he and those who were with him: how he entered the house of God and ate the showbread which was not lawful for him to eat, nor for those who were with him, but only for the priests? Or have you not read in the law that on the*

Sabbath the priests in the temple profane the Sabbath, and are blameless? Yet I say to you that in this place there is One greater than the temple. But if you had known what this means, "I desire mercy and not sacrifice," you would not have condemned the guiltless. For the Son of Man is Lord even of the Sabbath.'"

(Matthew 12:1–8)

In effect, Jesus said to the Pharisees, "You don't know what you're talking about, so stop judging my boys!" The Pharisees were only interested in the nitty gritty details of keeping the law – they had totally missed the principle God wanted to teach them. But Jesus was about to upset the religious authorities even more!

"Now when He had departed from there, He went into their synagogue. And behold, there was a man who had a withered hand. And they asked Him, saying, 'Is it lawful to heal on the Sabbath?' – that they might accuse Him.

Then He said to them, 'What man is there among you who has one sheep, and if it falls into a pit on the Sabbath, will not lay hold of it and lift it out? Of how much more value then is a man than a sheep? Therefore it is lawful to do good on the Sabbath.' Then He said to the man, 'Stretch out your hand.' And he stretched it out, and it was restored as whole as the other. Then the Pharisees went out and plotted against Him, how they might destroy Him." (Matthew 12:9–14)

Look how bad it becomes when you don't understand the premise for the Sabbath! How on earth, logically, could the Pharisees arrive at the conclusion that it is bad to do good on the Sabbath! How can it be a bad thing for God to heal the sick just because it is the Sabbath? If anything, what better day for healing to take place than on our "restoration" day! The legalistic application of the Sabbath principle actually tried to prevent Jesus from doing His ministry!

In Hebrews 4:9–10 the Bible says,

> *"There remains therefore a rest for the people of God. For he who has entered His rest has himself also ceased from his works as God did from His."*

The writer to the Hebrews understood that true "rest" in God's economy is not about conforming to a day, but about abiding in His presence. When it says, "he who has entered His rest has ceased from his labours" the writer isn't talking here about death, he is talking about ceasing from striving because we have found rest in the all-sufficiency of God. One of the reasons people work 24–7 is because they are *striving* – striving for a better house, a better car, a better life. Yet, ironically, if they had a day of rest and honoured God on that day they would get all the blessings they desired without striving! When you are resting in God you stop trying to make things happen for yourself and trust God to supply your needs. Then, even though we still have one day that is set apart for God, *every day* becomes a Sabbath and *every day* is a day of rest! We stop being driven and start being led.

If we don't understand the power of resting in God, nothing else we do will have any meaning. I can't understand people who say, "I haven't been to church for three weeks because I've been busy." Shame on them! They are eating stinking manna! God gives us six days and He asks us for one in return. He asks for a tenth of our income and let's us keep 90% of it, promising to bless it. Hebrews 4:7 says, *"Today if you hear His voice, do not harden your hearts."* "Today" might be the day when God wants to give you a Sabbath experience, to touch your life, bless you, release you, heal you or whatever it may be. Our understanding must go beyond a set day!

Finally, Colossians 2:16–17 says,

> *"Let no one judge you in food or in drink, or regarding a festival or a new moon or sabbaths, which are a shadow of things to come, but the substance is of Christ."*

In other words, all these laws are good, but they are only a shadow of the reality that is found and fulfilled in Christ. In Christ you know how to rest, how to worship, how to receive God's provision for your life. All the blessing of the Sabbath is contained in Christ. If we become men and women of the Sabbath God will meet all our needs and we will be blessed. Aren't you glad that not only is Sunday the Lord's day, but every day is the Lord's day?

Honour Your Father and Your Mother

*"Honour your father and your mother,
that your days may be long upon the land..."*
(Exodus 20:12)

This is one of the shortest of the Commandments and (which surprised me when I was I researching for this book) one of the least discussed by biblical commentators. Yet, it is a vitally important commandment and obedience to it, and conversely disobedience, has far reaching implications.

Deuteronomy 5:16 says:

> *"Honour your father and your mother, as the LORD your God has commanded you, that your days may be long, and that it may be well with you in the land which the LORD your God is giving you."*

In this chapter I am focusing on the principle of *honour* – what it means to honour God and honour our parents – and what it does *not* mean! The way in which we honour God and how we honour our parents are intrinsically linked. You cannot be properly honouring God if you are dishonouring your parents. First we will look at how we honour our "heavenly parent".

Honouring or dishonouring God?

When we think about God as our heavenly parent, it is interesting that He Himself decided to take on the title of "Father", though God is neither male nor female. People who harbour a feminist agenda are often offended by God calling Himself "Father" and they like to talk in terms of "Mother God" in an effort to be politically correct. Such a conversation totally misses the point as far as I'm concerned, since God does not have a personal sexuality. There must be another reason why God chose this title.

Man was made in God's image. God is an eternal Spirit and we have an eternal spirit. But we are clothed with flesh – our humanity. "Male" and "female" are purely human designations and the traits that both men and women uniquely possess are all attributes that belong to the one God. The spiritual characteristics that we posses – the desire to pray, to seek satisfaction and answers regarding the nature of life of earth and our purpose in it, questions about what will happen to us after death etc. – all of these are planted in us at birth because we bear the likeness of our Father. They are reflections of His nature because God has impregnated us with His life. Why did God choose to be called "Father" rather than "Mother"? I believe it is because it is the male in a relationship who imparts life by his seed. The female – the mother – then carries that life and nurtures it. God takes the title of "Father" to show that He is the instigator of life, the author of creation. It is not a sexist statement, but a creational one!

There are two main ways in which humanity seems consistently to dishonour God. Both constitute an attack on His very person. In what ways do we dishonour Him?

1. *By denying His unity.* There are many today who question the Trinity and in so doing dishonour the very essence of God's person. A characteristic of all major cults is a denial of the Trinity. Others, even some who would consider themselves to be orthodox Christians, simply cannot grasp the concept of the Trinity because they try to rationalise it in human terms instead of discerning it spiritually. To them, the idea that God could be "three personalities in one" is perplexing. They think that would make Him some kind of cosmic schizophrenic! But such arguments totally miss the point. God is Spirit and He is not bound by human constraints. Because God is Spirit He can be omnipresent, omniscient and omnipotent – and He can coexist as three independent yet harmonious persons in one. We cannot think of God as a man. He possesses attributes that are far above anything we can conceive of or understand. The members of the Trinity work together in beautiful harmony and that is why Jesus was so keen to teach the principle of unity when He was here on earth. It was unity that caused the Holy Spirit to fall on the disciples in the upper room. When people deny God's unity, they bring dishonour to His name and stem the flow of His blessing.

2. *By denying His deity.* Many people believe that Jesus was just a good man, but no more than that. If you ask a Muslim who Jesus is, he will tell you He is one of their prophets,

but he would not acknowledge Jesus beyond that. If you were to ask a Jehovah's Witness on your doorstep, "Do you believe Jesus is the Son of God?" he would say, "Yes." But he doesn't actually believe Jesus is "God the Son". All the major cults believe that Jesus is not on equal terms with the Father. They believe Jesus is a "lesser" God.

Why is this important and what does it have to do with honouring our earthly parents you may ask? It is important and relevant for this reason: God Himself dwells in unity as a "family unit" as demonstrated by the Trinity and this is His will for us. God wants there to be a unity between us and our parents. God knows that if there is an harmonious relationship between sons/daughters and their parents (just as there is an harmonious relationship between the Father and the Son and the Holy Spirit) then great blessing and fruitfulness will result. God has modelled family unity for us by showing us the wonder of the Trinity.

No other "religion" can grasp and understand this – it has to come by revelation. Then, the challenge that the cults bring to the deity of Christ and His equality with the Father is another glaring example of humanistic interpretation. It fails to see the significance and power of the unity of the Godhead and tries to dissociate Jesus from God – to separate the family unit. Most cults, when challenged about this doctrine, will quote Jesus' statement, "My Father is greater than I." But this is a simplistic and inaccurate interpretation of what Jesus said. In fact, Jesus is not "lesser" than the Father in any other sense than function. Jesus has a different function from the Father, but He possesses perfect equality.

All of this is important to us because the Bible reveals that

there is great blessing to be found in recognizing and acknowledging God *for who He is*. Acknowledging the deity of Christ and
accepting God's Fatherhood over our lives releases blessing and
it provides a model for us to emulate in our earthly relationships.

Matthew 16:13 tells the account of the moment when
Peter received revelation about who Jesus really was. We read
that,

> *"When Jesus came into the region of Caesarea Philippi, He
> asked His disciples, saying, 'Who do men say that I, the Son of
> Man, am?' "*

Jesus referred to Himself as the Son of Man because that's how
His disciples saw Him at that point – in the flesh as a man. But
He wanted them to receive the greater revelation of who He
really was in essence: the Son of God. In answer to His question
the disciples replied,

> *"Some say John the Baptist, some Elijah, and others Jeremiah or
> one of the prophets."*   (verse 14)

Jesus responded by asking them, *"But who do you say that I am?"*
(verse 15) and Peter answers Him in verse 16:

> *"You are the Christ, the Son of the living God."*

Then Jesus says,

> *"Blessed are you, Simon Bar-Jonah, for flesh and blood has not
> revealed this to you, but My Father who is in heaven."*
>   (verse 17)

After this exchange Jesus proceeded to talk to Peter about how He would be used by God to open up the kingdom. Isn't that incredible? Peter received this immense blessing and privilege just for making one statement. Peter was handed the keys to the kingdom and the honour of starting Christ's Church, not because of his intellectual abilities, his academic qualifications or his knowledge and wisdom, but purely because of the fact that, by revelation, Peter saw beyond the flesh of the man and acknowledged the attributes of God visible in Jesus. Peter honoured Jesus by recognizing His position. I say all this to say that here is a vital key to honouring our parents – we honour them purely because of the position they hold, for who they are in relation to us.

I will expand on that thought later in the chapter. For now, we understand that Peter saw in Jesus the divine DNA of His Father, the characteristics of Almighty God. He understood by revelation that Jesus was born of the Holy Ghost, not of Joseph the carpenter. It was a revelation that a simple fisherman could never have had other than it being supernaturally imparted by the Holy Spirit.

Jesus recognized and acknowledged the fact that His Father had imparted this knowledge to Peter, and it was at this point that Jesus knew he could entrust Peter with the task of being the first evangelist, the man who would plant the first church. More than that, Peter was given the authority and power to bind and release. Here is a principle for all of us: if we honour God He will release incredible resources to us. God rewards us not for our physical skills, but for our spiritual perception. This simple fisherman became pivotal in Christ establishing His Church and he was given the keys to unlock the power and provision of the Kingdom. The earth would now receive an abundance of blessing!

A picture of the model father

Jesus' whole mission on earth was to restore mankind to the level of relationship with God that was lost in the Fall; a relationship where God could be known as "Father", personally and intimately. Since Adam and Eve people had not known what it was to have a one-on-one relationship with God, let alone call Him "Father". Jesus, through His act of reconciliation on the cross, became the bridge that would reconnect mankind with God as Father. Now, through Christ, we can experience fully the Fatherhood of God.

Throughout the New Testament the relationship between Jesus and God the Father is the perfect example of fatherhood–sonship. Jesus, in many ways and on many different levels, was always demonstrating to people what His Father was like. In the prayer that He taught His disciples He highlighted one particular characteristic – forgiveness – and it is vital that we should grasp this.

The Lord's prayer says, "Forgive us our trespasses as we forgive those who trespass against us." Forgiveness, Jesus says, has to be an integral part of your relationship with the Father. In fact, our whole relationship with God is based on forgiveness. Forgiveness is at the heart of the Christian faith because God is a forgiving Father. So then we know that the heart of the perfect father is always rooted in forgiveness.

The apostle Paul taught that forgiveness was the key which unlocks the door of inheritance to us: "*. . . that they may receive forgiveness of sins **and an inheritance** among those who are sanctified by faith in* [Jesus]" (Acts 26:18, emphasis added). Under Jewish law, only a father was able to leave an inheritance for his children. We know that it is God's will that each of us inherits all the blessing and provision He has for us through Christ. Forgiveness is the door we must walk through to reach that provision.

All of this serves to further enhance our picture of God the Father and it paints a picture of how earthly parents should behave. We realize that God's nature is *to forgive and to reward*. Regardless of how your earthly parents treated you, God's heart towards you is to forgive and to reward. God is not sitting in Heaven waiting to slap you around the head and send you to hell! God is a rewarder of those who diligently seek Him.

The commandment with a legacy

Paul spells out for us in Ephesians that this commandment has a legacy attached to it:

> " 'Honour your father and mother,' **which is the first commandment with promise:** 'that it may be well with you and you may live long on the earth.' "
>
> (Ephesians 6:2–3, emphasis added)

God literally promises us that if we honour our father and mother we will live longer than we might otherwise have done and have more of a blessed life than we ever anticipated. Isn't that incredible? What a promise!

It seems to me, however, that people have tended to fall into two traps when it comes to honouring their parents. On the one hand, some people have deferred to their parents to the point where it has become unhealthy – allowing themselves to be dominated and manipulated. Or, on the other hand, they have forgotten and ignored their parents and tried to live a prosperous life independently of them. God's plan, however, is that we don't just live our lives independently. We have to fulfil His rules in order to be truly blessed, and His rules include honouring our parents as a key to releasing His provision in our lives. When you are young, you have to obey your parents because they have authority and responsibility for you. While you are under your parents' care, obedience is necessary. As adults we are called to *honour* our parents, which is different from *obeying* them.

Honouring our parents

We have now reached a critical point in our journey – the point where we have to think about "honour" in relation to our earthly parents and not just our heavenly Father. Most Christians can appreciate the fact that God is a perfect Father with our wellbeing at heart, though some struggle even with this truth. But what of our relationship with our earthly mum and dad? Some readers may be saying, "Don't go any further. I never knew my father . . . I've never met my mother . . . I was adopted . . . my father abused me . . ." Please bear with me as we continue this journey together. Don't switch off, because it could change your life!

Your father/mother may have treated you appallingly, or, indeed, you may never have had a real relationship with them. But this does not prevent you from obeying this commandment and enjoying the rewards of God for doing so. First of all, we must remember that *to honour does not mean to obey*. Some people had fathers who beat them or who were perverts. Some people had mothers who were prostitutes or alcoholics. God doesn't expect us to "obey" anyone who lives an ungodly lifestyle, totally contrary to the Bible. Yet, paradoxically, if the description fits your father/mother you can still "honour" them. How? By acknowledging their "position" and "function" as your parent. Honour means "to make glorious ... to speak for ... to promote ... to act honourably towards..." At the very least, you can honour your parents by not dishonouring them i.e. by not speaking ill of them, by not putting them down, by not treating them with contempt.

Avoiding dishonouring your parents is important for the following reason. This is something God really spoke to me about as I was praying and thinking about it. What He said was a revelation to me: as an individual you are made up from two-thirds your parents and one-third yourself. You carry the DNA of your parents and you have a part which is uniquely you. Whenever you dishonour your parents, therefore, *you dishonour yourself* and when you dishonour yourself you deny who you are – your very DNA! Conversely, when you honour your parents you release something in yourself.

My wife, Molly, due to family circumstances, was separated from her younger brother and didn't see him for forty-two years. When they were finally reunited it was amazing to see that they shared so many characteristics in common. Both had suffered from a tumour in the same place on the same ankle. Both had a very low tolerance to the cold. They shared lots of similar traits because they had the same father and shared his DNA. Molly has never tried to be like her dad, but the fact is, she is part of her dad and he is part of her. It's in her DNA.

The honouring of parents is a principle which has come under increasing stress in recent times, chiefly because we have allowed ourselves to create a societal culture where dishonour and rebellion have been allowed to flourish unchecked. The family unit has been constantly besieged over many years and is constantly under threat. All this adds up to the fact that the respect and deference that fathers and mothers once automatically enjoyed has been greatly diminished. Society has spawned a generation of young people who react badly to leadership and authority because they have had so little experience of it! This stands in stark contrast to the model relationship of Jesus and Father God. Jesus' whole life was founded on His relationship with His Father. He only ever did what He saw His Father doing and He only said what He heard His Father saying. Jesus was always talking about His Father and His big house – like a kid bragging about how great his dad is! Jesus talked about His Father all the time.

Our earthly parents are not always worthy of such honour, but nevertheless we can and should respect their position. Even if we strongly disagree with our parents we can honour them in much the same way we would "honour" the Queen or a prominent politician. Whether you believe the UK should have a monarchy or not, if you met the Queen you would treat her with respect. Similarly, if Tony Blair turned up at our Sunday morning church service next week, rather than pouncing on him and telling him what a mess he made of the Iraq conflict, I would honour his former position as the political leader of our nation and treat him with respect. That is not being two-faced, it is honouring his position as the Bible instructs me to!

People often tell me, "I can't honour my dad for what he's done." But, with respect, I reply, "Yes, you can. You can honour his position, if not his actions." Whether you had good parents or bad ones you can at least honour them for this: *they gave you life.* Apart from their union you would not exist today! Whilst there may not be much that you can honour your parents for, you can honour them for that.

A lady came to me once and said, "My dad has rejected me; he doesn't want to see me. How can I honour him?" I said to her, "Do you know you are an attractive lady?" which disarmed her somewhat and she smiled at me. I said to her, "Go home and look in the mirror and tell yourself, 'Without my dad I could have been ugly', because your dad helped you look like that." The statement took her by surprise, but she understood the point! We don't honour our parents for the things they do, but because of their position. If we reject them, we reject ourselves.

Often it is necessary to forgive your parents for their actions, because all parents are dysfunctional to a greater or lesser degree. There is no such thing as a perfect parent! If you don't forgive your parents you dishonour them and very often the negative traits which you so despise will end up overcoming you. The end result is that you become like your parents and find yourself doing all those things that they did that you hated! Dishonour sets that cycle in motion. If you honour your parents, God can redeem all the negatives and turn them into positives. You can become the person your parents longed to become. We have to do this, at the very least, because God says, "How can you love Me if you don't love your parents? How can you say you honour Me when you won't honour them?"

Your parents may have failed you, but in Christ you can become what your parents failed to become. Perhaps your dad committed adultery and ran off with someone else, abandoning you and your mother? You have some of his DNA, but in Christ you don't have to be what he was. Plus you can become what he could never be. You are not doomed to fail morally in the same way. Instead you can become what your father could have been in Christ. Maybe you had good parents? Well, all the good they possessed God can take and make better still in you. The Bible says that curses last four generations, but blessings last for thousands of generations.

Cutting emotional cords

As an aside, it is worth mentioning in more detail an issue I alluded to earlier. There are those people who, for whatever reason, go to extremes in honouring their parents and find themselves being manipulated emotionally. This is often due to parents who refuse to "release" their children into maturity. There comes a time when sons and daughters grow up, mature and leave home. This is the time when the parents should cut the "umbilical cord", metaphorically speaking, for the second time. The umbilical cord is a good analogy: whilst a child is in the womb the cord keeps it alive. It is the baby's sole source of nutrients. But once the child is born the cord must be severed or what once sustained the child will kill it. When a child is growing up and developing they do so in the environment of their parents' home and there is a strong emotional bond and attachment. Once the child has matured and is ready to leave the family home, however, the parents must "cut" the emotional cord and embark on a new level of relationship with their child. It is as different as a baby transitioning from the umbilical cord to the breast. By releasing their children a second time, parents end up "keeping" them. Some parents refuse to cut the emotional cord and end up suffocating their children and turning them away. The principle to remember is: let go of anything that loves you and it will come back. I believe this whole process is vitally important in enabling children to honour their parents. The parent who nurtures and protects their children, and then releases them into maturity, recognizing them as adults in their own right, will certainly be honoured and respected.

A personal illustration

I want to end this chapter with a personal illustration. My dad, Bert, though he wasn't a Christian at the time, believed in honouring his parents, despite the fact that circumstances and people made it very difficult for him to do so. This is the briefest of sketches of his story:

My dad was a good man and I really loved him. He was small in stature and my mum was small too. I've no idea how they produced me and my brothers, one of whom is 6′ 4″! Go back with me eighty years to a time when my grandmother had £40,000 in the bank. It was the equivalent of millions today. My dad was coming up to eighteen. He had a wealthy uncle who had few relatives and drove around in a Rolls Royce. He approached his sister and said, "I want to put your Albert through university because he's a bright lad." My grandmother refused and said, "He will go to work at Cadbury's factory like all the other lads. I'm not going to do anything special for him." This uncle eventually died and all his money went to other relatives. My dad should have benefited from that, but he got nothing.

My dad, who wasn't a Christian, was a man's man. He worked a sixty-hour week at Cadbury's. During the war he lived quite a distance away from his mother, but nevertheless he would walk to her house to visit her every Saturday. She was so hostile towards him that very often she wouldn't even answer the door, leaving him standing on the doorstep. She would watch him through the window until he gave up waiting, turned around and walked home. Friends used to ask him, "Bert, why would you do that for such a woman?" and he would always answer, "The Bible says 'honour your father and mother'."

Years later, when Dad was sixty years old, not long after Molly and I were married, I got a call from Mum. I was on my way to do business in Coventry when I decided, on the spur of the moment, to pop home to pick something up. While I was there the phone rang and Mum told me that Dad didn't look well. Despite being busy, I felt God saying I should go over and see him, so I cancelled my appointment and drove straight over there. When I walked in and saw my dad he looked terrible. Dad, of course, was the same as ever, "Oh, it's your mother fussing over me. I'm alright." But I knew he had either had a heart attack or was about to have one because his lips were blue. We got him into hospital straight away and as soon as he arrived there he did have a heart attack. He would have died had I not gone over there to see him. My dad became a Christian whilst he was in hospital and lived for another eighteen years. I believe that God blessed him with a longer life because he honoured the woman who, for reasons best known to her, despised him.

God lengthened my dad's life, but what prosperity did He give my dad for obeying His Word? He was, after all, just a charge hand at a chocolate factory for forty-six years. He could potentially have become a business tycoon if his mother had not denied him her brother's finance and mentoring. Because of the circumstances of his life and the animosity of his mother he could easily have become a bitter man. No one in his life ever encouraged him. Yet, God gave my dad an incredible heritage. The day he died we discovered he had left a taped message for my mum. When we listened to it we realized that Dad must have known he was going. On the tape he said, "Winnie, we're getting old now. I've never had much, but I love you more now than I did when you had golden hair. But I have produced three preachers..."

Every one of Albert Carr's sons is a minister of the Gospel. What a great inheritance from God! Because of Dad's faithful, steadfast attitude to life, thousands of others' lives have been changed, countless lives saved. Because he honoured his parents, great blessing was released through his life. Although his mother was a bitter woman, Dad never dishonoured her. She didn't control his life, but he respected her and visited her faithfully, honouring her till the day she died. That is the power of honour.

What dreams were locked up in your father or mother that they never achieved? All those dreams can be unlocked and activated in you by God if you honour your parents – only it will be ten times better than if your parents had done it. Don't dishonour and reject your parents, not matter what kind of relationship you have had with them. Honour them and God will honour you.

You Shall Not Murder ... You Shall Not Steal

"You shall not murder ... You shall not steal."
(Exodus 20:13, 15)

Murder

Exodus 20:13 says simply, *"You shall not murder."* Murder is the act of taking an innocent person's life without cause. It is different and distinct from "killing" someone – an act which may take place through reason of war or entirely by accident (known as manslaughter in legal terms: the unlawful killing of one human by another without express or implied intent to do injury). The Old Testament observes this difference between murder and killing. David was rewarded in 1 Samuel 17 for killing Goliath. By doing so he received the hand of the king's daughter and knew the favour of God. In spiritual terms David, who had been anointed by Samuel as future king of Israel, was destroying the powers of darkness that were mocking the nation of Israel and he was elevated by that act.

However, the same man, David, was punished by God in 2 Samuel 11 for the death of Uriah the Hittite. (This story is covered in more detail in the chapter on adultery and is also mentioned in the chapter on covetousness.) David had Uriah murdered so that he would not stand in the way of David's affair with his wife. Two men died by the hand of David – one of which he was rewarded for and the other which he was punished for. There was a distinct difference and that difference was the motivation of the heart.

Similarly, Moses led the children of Israel into many battles and in the process killed many of Israel's foes. But the same man earlier had to flee into hiding when he murdered an Egyptian who was cruelly oppressing his people. There was a difference between Moses lifting his hand against Israel's enemies under the anointing of God and Moses lifting his hand against an Egyptian oppressor of his own volition and murdering him because of his anger.

God singled out "murder" to include in His Ten Commandments, but like all of the Commandments its scope is wide-ranging. Elsewhere God made it clear that He was against any kind of violence which was perpetrated against the innocent. Exodus 21:12–26 lists several commands designed to deal with the inappropriate use of violence in general. Amongst these commands Exodus 21:14 stands out. It says,

> *"If a man acts with premeditation against his neighbour, to kill him by treachery, you shall take him from My altar, that he may die."*

The key word here is "premeditation". Again it underlines the fact that it is the *heart motive* that leads to sin.

The remaining commands in this section of Scripture deal with a number of acts that could endanger human life through carelessness. Deuteronomy chapter 22 takes up a similar theme. Deuteronomy 22:8 says,

> *"When you build a new house, then you shall make a parapet for your roof, that you may not bring guilt of bloodshed on your household if anyone falls from it."*

This verse amazed me when I first read it. The exact same law has only just been introduced in Europe and the UK is one of the few countries currently enforcing it. When we built a small chapel next door to our main church building we had to spend £23,000 putting a rail all round the edge in case somebody fell off. What someone would be doing up there in the first place is another question, but the fact is, if someone fell from our roof we would be in trouble – unless we had a safety rail. God in His wisdom and foresight takes account of such things long before they occur to us!

As well as raising the issue of death through carelessness, the Bible also cautions against "wantonness". In other words, gratuitous acts of treachery against our fellow human beings. There are many examples I could list but Leviticus 19:17–18 says,

> *"You shall not hate your brother in your heart. You shall surely rebuke your neighbour, and not bear sin because of him. You shall not take vengeance, nor bear any grudge against the children of your people, but you shall love your neighbour as yourself: I am the LORD."*

This tells us that God includes under the overall banner of "murder" such acts as hatred, anger and revenge. Jesus applied this truth in His own teaching. He said,

> *"You have heard that it was said to those of old, 'You shall not murder, and whoever murders will be in danger of the judgment.' But I say to you that whoever is angry with his brother without a cause shall be in danger of the judgment."*
>
> (Matthew 5:21–22)

We have noted elsewhere in this book that none of the commandments are independent of one another. If you violate one commandment you are liable to violate them all. This commandment, as with all of the last six, is concerned with how we violate the basic human rights of our fellow beings.

When you covet your neighbour's goods you violate the validity of his ownership. God has allowed our neighbour to own what he owns and we should rejoice with him. We shouldn't crave for it or lust after it. It's not ours! To bear false witness is to violate the validity of another person's credibility. To murder someone is to violate the very validity of their existence. It is to no longer believe that they have any place in this life. But Jesus taught that we commit similar violations when we harbour feelings of anger, bitterness, resentment, jealously and hatred towards others. By doing this we are just as guilty of breaking God's Commandments.

There are Christians walking around today who turn up to church every Sunday but have no joy in their life. In fact, a dead donkey would have more joy! Why? Because they have killed it. They have killed the joy of the Lord because of their attitude towards others; by harbouring ill feeling. The Bible says that in the presence of God there is fullness of joy, so where God's presence is absent then there is no joy. The joy of the Lord is our strength and if we have no joy then we are spiritually weak.

Jesus teaching in Matthew chapter 5 shows that the Christian should not live like this! The believer, empowered by the Holy Spirit, is called to live at a higher level than merely observing the law. Jesus' expectation is that we should transcend the law and live beyond what society has grown to expect. In Christ God has shown us clearly that spiritual antagonism is akin to physical murder. We have as good as murdered a person when we want to see them brought down and defeated. What was once defined as guilty by action is now guilty by intent.

Jesus went on to teach the principle of reconciliation. He says in Matthew 5:23–24,

> *"If you bring your gift to the altar, and there remember that your brother has something against you, leave your gift there before the altar, and go your way. First be reconciled to your brother, and then come and offer your gift."*

And again, this time speaking of a disagreement that leads to court action, Jesus said,

> *"Agree with your adversary quickly, while you are on the way with him, lest your adversary deliver you to the judge, the judge hand you over to the officer, and you be thrown into prison."*
> (Matthew 5:25)

Essentially Jesus was warning us, "If you live like the world, think like the world and talk like the world, you will receive the world's punishment." We must not let our attitudes and emotions get so out of control that we begin to think murderous thoughts, for this, Jesus says, is the place where murder originates – in our heart. The heart, the mind and the mouth, according to God, are the real weapons of assassination. You can kill someone in your mind and dismiss them as worthless. You can kill their credibility by what you think about them. You can kill their reputation by what you say about them.

Instead, we need to work at maintaining right heart attitudes towards one another. This isn't just a good idea, but God's mandate for us.

Stealing

Murder, theft, covetousness, false witness are all violations of the destiny of others. To steal is as much targeted at God as it is man. When we do these things we do them against God, not just against other people. How do we steal from God? Malachi 3:8–9 says:

> *"Will a man rob God?*
> *Yet you have robbed Me!*
> *But you say,*
> *'In what way have we robbed You?'*
> *In tithes and offerings.*
> *You are cursed with a curse* [you are limited with a limit].*"*

God says that if we steal from Him then He can't bless us. It's not that He is sulking. It's just the law of sowing and reaping. You are cursed with poverty over your life when you lie and cheat and steal. In the New Testament Ananias and Sapphira did that and died.

We live in the New Testament. God says, Don't make a promise you won't fulfil. If you make a pledge to your church building fund, don't do it unless you intend to honour it. If you do you are heaping judgement on yourself. Better not to make the pledge. God doesn't give you any way out other than righteousness and righteousness builds a nation up. Too many people make vows to God that they then don't honour. We need to ask God to forgive us when we renege on promises we have made to Him. He takes them very seriously.

So God says honour Me and don't lie to Me and don't steal from Me and I will bless you. God is not refusing to bless you because you steal. It is that by stealing you are stopping Him from blessing you. God's whole heart is to bless you. The only thing that stops Him is our breaking of the Commandments. God is committed to blessing you until you stop Him. So often we act as if we don't know why God has blessed us. "Oh, I'm so surprised, God has blessed me with this. I've no idea why!" We should not be surprised! When we say those things what are we doing? We are waiting for someone to say, "Oh, it's because you're good." No, that's not it. God blesses us even though we are not good in ourselves. He blesses all those who are in Christ who obey His Commandments. It is human thinking to associate God's blessing on our lives with our actions – the supposed good things we have done.

We're not good. Any parent wants to bless their children. God knows us, knows what we need and He blesses us abundantly above and beyond our needs. But you remove privileges from your children when they sin against you. "Until you can learn to say sorry, I am stopping your pocket money." That's what you do. God is the same. He cannot and will not reward disobedience. Some people will let their kids do anything and they still reward them. That's bad parenting.

Isaiah 10:1–3 says,

> *"Woe to those who decree unrighteous decrees,*
> *Who write misfortune,*
> *Which they have prescribed*
> *To rob the needy of justice,*
> *And to take what is right from the poor of My people,*
> *That the widows may be their prey,*
> *And that they may rob the fatherless.*
> *What will you do in the day of punishment . . .*
> *To whom will you flee for help? . . . "*

God says if you steal from the poor, widows and the fatherless I will get you! That's why in our church we have Helping Hands. Con men who go around conning old people out of their money will not ultimately get away with it. Isn't God a God of grace when He sees three vulnerable groups of people – those who are genuinely poor, those who are widows, those who are struggling? – and God says My eye is on these people. I see them. Don't you dare steal from them.

In the New Testament, Romans 2:21–22 says,

> *"You, therefore, who teach another, do you not teach yourself?*
> *You who preach that a man should not steal, do you steal? You*
> *who say, 'Do not commit adultery,' do you commit adultery?*
> *You who abhor idols, do you rob temples?"*

This is for leaders. Paul says it is no good being the preacher of a good sermon unless you live it! Every time I sit down to write a sermon God speaks to me first! The world is fed up with people who are good preachers, who get good fees for travelling around speaking and stay in good hotels, but who don't live good lives! People who live like that are stealing God's glory. If you preach fidelity and yet commit adultery, then people will not believe God any more. If you aspire to be a preacher then you better realize that you have to walk your talk. Because, God says, otherwise you are stealing.

Exodus 22:3 says that every sin is forgivable but it has a consequence. If you steal you must restore. We don't hear this preached today. The law on theft was that you restored at least double to the person you stole from.

> *"Let him who stole steal no longer, but rather let him labour, working with his hands what is good, that he may have something to give him who has need."*   (Ephesians 4:28)

You must learn to pay back.

Jeremiah 23:30 says,

> *" 'Therefore behold, I am against the prophets,' says the LORD, 'who steal My words every one from his neighbour.' "*

We are for the gifts of the Spirit in our church, but we try to protect people and test any prophecies that are given for this reason: if they are wrong it is stealing from God. There are single women who have had someone prophesy over them in some meeting, "Your husband is on the horizon." If this doesn't come true the "prophecy" has devalued the word of God in those people's hearts. They begin to doubt and think, "Did God really say . . . ?" It shakes their faith and makes them think, "Can I continue to trust God for this?"

The Commandments, like the gifts of the Spirit and their fruit, are seldom independent. Zacchaeus in Luke 19:8 said this about stealing, *"Then Zacchaeus stood and said to the Lord, 'Look, Lord, I give half of my goods to the poor . . . I restore fourfold . . . "*

That was the law. He only fulfilled the law. If we steal from people – physically, emotionally, mentally, spiritually – we've got to pay them back. It's payback time! Go and serve them. Go and do something. Don't say, "God's forgiven me now and it's not a problem any more." Yes, it is!

Numbers 5 speaks of restitution. Much is spoken of restoration, regeneration, righteousness, but little today of restitution. Yet it was this action which prompted Jesus to say to this one man only, *"Today salvation has come to this house"* (Luke 19:9).

The Beatitudes

In closing I mention the Beatitudes, which means "blessings". These are the graces that accompany the Commandments when applied by one who is born of God and filled with the Holy Spirit.

When Jesus said the Ten Commandments now are going to be lived out through grace, this is what accompanies keeping the Ten Commandments – His blessing. His blessing breaks curses.

- *Blessed are the poor in spirit* – those who are no longer going to live in pride and personal promotion. What's in it for me? I've been sitting in this church for six months and no one has asked me to do anything. They don't appreciate my ministry. Always looking for a reward etc.

- *Blessed are they who mourn* – does this mean we go around crying all the time? No. It means those who understand their relationship with God and realize that sin grieves Him, not those who spend their life eating, drinking and being merry and turn up on a Sunday. What happens to those who mourn? – they are comforted. Wouldn't it be wonderful for Christians to live in the comfort of God? We have a Comforter who is the Holy Spirit.

- *Blessed are the meek* – this does not mean the "weak", but those not obsessed with power. The promise to the meek is to inherit the earth. Those who are truly meek are rewarded by God. They are the ones who will have the big churches, successful businesses, etc., because they are not craving those things. God can trust them with much.

- *Blessed are the righteous* – those people with no hidden agendas are filled with satisfaction. People often ask me what I want for my birthday or Christmas. I never know because there is nothing I want. I'm satisfied.

- *Blessed are the merciful* – those with strength, yet with the compassion and sensitivity not to squash people. One day I spent counselling, everyone who turned up had a mental issue of some kind, which can be very draining. I just put my arms around each of them and told them, "I love you." If God didn't sustain our minds in this world we live in, any one of us could be in that position. We need to be more merciful. The reward for mercy is mercy, God forgives our sins when we are merciful towards others.

- *Blessed are the poor in heart* – those who are not deceitful – they shall see God!

- *Blessed are the peacemakers* – not those who get a name for brokering peace treaties around the world, but those who do it without ever getting mentioned. They shall be called sons and daughters of God.

- *Blessed are they who are persecuted* – not through being abusive! Some people say to me, "Pastor Dave, I get persecuted at work." I want to say to them, "Yes, it's because you're obnoxious! You're rude and lazy!" If you are persecuted, make sure it's because you are right-eous, not because you're a pain. What's the reward? The kingdom of God. We are going to inherit it. Jesus has gone to prepare a place for us. Where He is, we shall be also.

We have a greater level of blessing than those who lived under Law. We who live in the love that the Commandments generate through the knowledge of Christ Jesus are custodians of His grace. Do we love God with all our heart, mind, soul and strength? Do we love ourselves? Do we really love our neighbours . . . our enemies? Remember, in the words of the gurus of the 70s, money can't buy you love. But seek first the kingdom of God and His righteousness and everything else you need will be added unto you.

You Shall Not Commit Adultery

"You shall not commit adultery."
(Exodus 20:14)

Exodus 20:14 states simply and unequivocally, *"You shall not commit adultery."* Here God highlights a straightforward and vitally important principle regarding our relationships. Remembering that the original purpose of the Ten Commandments was to reveal the nature of God to mankind, what does this statement tell us? That God is a *faithful* God. He is not adulterous. This tells us a lot about what God will do and what He won't do. The fact that God is not adulterous enables Him to speak promises such as,

> *"The LORD, He is the One who goes before you. He will be with you, He will not leave you nor forsake you; do not fear nor be dismayed."*   (Deuteronomy 31:8)

And,

> *"I will not leave you nor forsake you."*   (Joshua 1:5)

Once we are in relationship with God He never leaves us, never abandons us to fend for ourselves. He is a faithful and unchanging God. God places a very high value on faithfulness, which is what makes adultery so bad. Adultery is a betrayal of trust, a breaking of faithfulness. Most people realize that adultery is a bad thing and that we shouldn't do it, but they tend to think only of the area of sexual infidelity. Even non-Christian people know, deep down, that it is wrong to be unfaithful to your husband or wife by having sex with someone else. But adultery is more than that. Adultery is not just a physical act, but a spiritual one. It is not just a sin that is committed against your husband/wife, it is an act of violation committed against God. Adultery has spiritual implications, which is why God places this principle clearly in the midst of all the other Commandments.

It has been said that the Commandments can be divided into two halves: those that are towards God and those that are towards humanity and our relations with one another. This is true to a point, in the sense that we outwork the laws of God towards and with one another, but I would like to suggest that all ten of the Commandments are seeded in our relationship with God because each one is a spiritual principle before it is a physical reality. The commandment we are examining here has obvious consequences upon human relationships, but it has deep spiritual consequences too.

Of all the Commandments, this one is probably the most emotive. Many churches and their ministers studiously avoid speaking about adultery or teaching on it. And yet, you don't need to be an expert on statistics to work out that an increasing number of people are becoming either victims of or instigators of adultery. In the UK alone, 69% of divorces are granted to women, 52% of which are granted because of the husband's "behaviour". My purpose here, however, is not to approach the topic in a legalistic way that will bring people into condemnation. Instead, we need to get inside this commandment and understand what was in the heart of God when He gave it. All the Commandments are given for our benefit, health and blessing.

Can adultery be forgiven?

Before we progress further, I can say as a minister of many years, that one question that seems to be paramount in the minds of many is, "Can adultery be forgiven?" A second question might be, "Can someone who has committed adultery ever be used by God again?" The answer to both questions is, I believe, most definitely, yes. Adultery is not the unforgivable sin and some Christians need to hear that. Any sin that is truly repented of before God can be forgiven, but we need to remember that every sin has consequences. If you commit murder you can be forgiven by God, but you still have to serve an appropriate prison term in accordance with your crime. God has forgiven you, but you then have to fulfil the law because the sin was not only committed in spirit, but in flesh. So, yes, adultery can be forgiven. Can someone be used of God again after committing and repenting of this sin? My answer is yes, but ... The caveat here is: Has the person taken steps to make restitution where possible? Let me explain:

The Bible says that someone who has been a thief can be forgiven, but that that person should seek to make recompense for their crimes. The biblical mandate is that they should restore what was stolen fourfold. Technically speaking, if a person has led a life of thieving and debauchery and they become a Christian, they should spend their foreseeable future making right their wrongs, to the best of their ability. Zacchaeus, the corrupt tax collector, is an illustration of this Old Testament law in the New Testament. When he encounters Jesus and has his life transformed we see Zacchaeus doing two things: first, he says, "I will give half of my wealth to the poor." That was nothing to do with his guilt and conviction over his crimes, that was sheer generosity. Secondly, he said, "If I have wronged any man I will give back fourfold." That was not a number that Zacchaeus plucked out of the air, it was a Jewish law that he knew he had to fulfil.

Forgiveness sparks restitution, yet you seldom hear restitution preached today. At one meeting where I spoke about this, a former criminal came to me and thanked me. He told me, "I became a Christian in prison. I used to steal from old people. I couldn't believe God would ever forgive me for that, but He did. I've always felt, however, reading the Bible, that I should go out, get a job, and work hard until I've repaid every penny I stole from those old people – and give them a bonus." I told him he was absolutely right to do what he was doing. Other Christians had told him, "That's stupid. You don't have to bother with that; it's all under the blood."

I say all this to make this point: people cannot commit adultery and then walk away with impunity. There are often serious consequences that need to be dealt with and, if the person who has committed this sin wants to reach a place of wholeness, they should take this seriously. Imagine the following scenario: suppose a married man has an adulterous affair and conceives a child with someone. Some time later he becomes a Christian. What should he do? Some may say, "That happened in his former life outside of Christ, so it's history now." I don't believe that is what the Bible teaches. God has forgiven that man for his immoral lifestyle and for committing adultery, but the fact is, an innocent child came out of that union. It is the man's responsibility to pay for that child, educate it and love it until he / she is independent. That is what a real Christian should do. Christians don't walk away from their responsibilities. The only exception, in this scenario, would be if the man went back to the person he had the affair with, explained that he had become a Christian and wanted to do right by them and their child, and the woman involved did not want to know, refusing his assistance. The important thing is that the man made the offer to make things right – that is restitution. If we, the people of God, led the way in such issues, perhaps the world would follow. If the world could see that people in the Church own up to their responsibilities, the world would say, "Well, it works for the Church."

King David: a biblical case study

The Bible provides us with an in-depth look at the anatomy of adultery and it should be a salutary lesson to us. David, one of the Bible's great heroes, the famous warrior-poet-worshipper-musician, with a heart after God's own, surprisingly initiates an adulterous relationship with dire consequences. It seems that David, despite following the Lord passionately, was not immune from temptation and this should tell us something about ourselves – we are all vulnerable. The person who thinks they are not vulnerable to temptation in this area is perhaps the most vulnerable of all. David's adultery caused him to become tangled up in a web of deception and deceit. This grim case study is found in 2 Samuel chapters 11 and 12.

David was a very successful man of God. He had risen to a notable position in the land and he already had a beautiful wife whom he had won by killing the giant Goliath on behalf of the king at that time, Saul, who offered his daughter's hand in marriage to the man who would rid him of the Philistine. How do I know that Saul's daughter was exceptionally good looking, you may ask? Put it like this: you don't go out and try to kill a giant for an ugly woman! She must have been gorgeous! That being the case, what on earth went wrong with this marriage? David eventually became king himself. He had fame, fortune, position and a beautiful wife. Who could ask for more?

Yet, one of the most vulnerable times in a person's life is when they are successful; when everything seems to be going well. Why is this? Because when things are tough and dangerous we tend to guard ourselves. Self-preservation kicks in and we watch what we are doing. When everything seems to be going well we often become careless. We don't guard ourselves in the same way and, despite our success, we open ourselves up for the enemy to attack. The verses at the beginning of 2 Samuel 11 are very telling:

> "It happened in the spring of the year, at the time when kings go out to battle, that David sent Joab and his servants with him, and all Israel; and they destroyed the people of Ammon and besieged Rabbah. But David remained at Jerusalem. Then it happened one evening that David arose from his bed and walked on the roof of the king's house. And from the roof he saw a woman bathing, and the woman was very beautiful to behold. So David sent and inquired about the woman."
>
> (2 Samuel 11:1–3)

These verses paint the picture of a man who had become complacent. "At the time when kings go out to battle," David was at home. He sent others to fight his battles for him while he remained in Jerusalem. As the king he should have been leading his troops into battle, exhorting and encouraging them; showing them that their king, and therefore God Himself, was with them. Then one night, perhaps when he least expects it, David sees a lovely young woman bathing. She is unaware of his presence, but he watches her. The tragedy is, he really shouldn't have been there in the first place, but David gazes upon Bathsheba and he begins to lust.

The next thing we know is that this man of God has committed adultery. Before long he hears that Bathsheba is pregnant with his child. Then, the Bible says that David tries to cover up what has happened by summoning Bathsheba's husband from the battle front and attempting to orchestrate events so that he will sleep with his wife. In other words, David hoped that Uriah, her husband, would think the resulting baby was his own. But because this plot fails, David resorts to more desperate measures and makes sure that Joab, the commander of his army, places Uriah in a battle situation that will result in his death. David is now complicit in murder, as well as adultery.

I honestly believe that if you had said to David the day before he committed adultery with Bathsheba and this tragic sequence of events was put into motion, that he would be capable of such a thing, he would have drawn his sword and struck you dead. But David's complacency and therefore his vulnerability led him to this place. Very few people, unless they are seriously perverted, actually go out deliberately looking to commit the act.

Inevitably, of course, God confronted David with what he had done. Nathan the prophet was the individual tasked with delivering the word of the Lord to him. But instead of confronting him head on with the facts, the Lord first of all gave Nathan a parable to tell:

> *"There were two men in one city, one rich and the other poor. The rich man had exceedingly many flocks and herds. But the poor man had nothing, except one little ewe lamb which he had bought and nourished; and it grew up together with him and with his children. It ate of his own food and drank from his own cup and lay in his bosom; and it was like a daughter to him. And a traveller came to the rich man, who refused to take from his own flock and from his own herd to prepare one for the wayfaring man who had come to him; but he took the poor man's lamb and prepared it for the man who had come to him."*
>
> (2 Samuel 12:1–4)

David, who in the biblical account seems to think that Nathan is referring to literal events, gets angry when he hears about this act of selfishness:

> *"David's anger was greatly aroused against the man, and he said to Nathan, 'As the LORD lives, the man who has done this shall surely die! And he shall restore fourfold for the lamb, because he did this thing and because he had no pity.'"*
>
> (2 Samuel 12:5–6)

Then Nathan drops the bombshell: *"You are the man!"* he says (verse 7), and then he proceeds to tell David what God has to say about the matter.

> *"Thus says the LORD God of Israel: 'I anointed you king over Israel, and I delivered you from the hand of Saul. I gave you your*

master's house and your master's wives into your keeping, and
gave you the house of Israel and Judah. And if that had been too
little, I also would have given you much more! Why have you
despised the commandment of the LORD, to do evil in His sight?
You have killed Uriah the Hittite with the sword; you have
taken his wife to be your wife, and have killed him with the
sword of the people of Ammon. Now therefore, the sword shall
never depart from your house, because you have despised Me,
and have taken the wife of Uriah the Hittite to be your wife.'
Thus says the LORD: 'Behold, I will raise up adversity against
you from your own house; and I will take your wives before your
eyes and give them to your neighbour, and he shall lie with
your wives in the sight of this sun. For you did it secretly, but I
will do this thing before all Israel, before the sun.' ''

(2 Samuel 12:7–12)

David admits his guilt and confesses his sin. Notice that he
immediately realizes, *"I have sinned against the LORD"* (verse 13).
Nathan then tells David that God has forgiven his sin, but
announces a further consequence of his actions:

"The LORD also has put away your sin; you shall not die.
However, because by this deed you have given great occasion to
the enemies of the LORD to blaspheme, the child also who is born
to you shall surely die."   (2 Samuel 12:13–14)

One of the most significant aspects of this story is God's rebuke
of David. In it the Lord links the spiritual with the physical. God
connects the issue of adultery with the fact that David was living
under His anointing. In verse 7, God says, in effect, "Why did
you do this when you are an anointed person, set apart for Me?"

Sex, as we will see as we progress, is a physical representation of a spiritual reality. Sex is not just a physical act, it is the seal on a holy covenant created before God. When a person commits adultery they do so, first of all, in the realm of the spirit because they violate their covenant with God before they violate their covenant with their wife/husband. God wanted to know, firstly, why David had violated his covenant with Himself. "You know that I do not commit adultery," God might have said. "I have never been unfaithful to you, so why are you being unfaithful to Me?" Once we are in a covenantal relationship with God He never changes His mind about us.

Every time a leading man of God, like David, commits adultery he makes a laughing stock of the Gospel in front of the world. If I committed adultery next week – and I am not too proud to admit that it is possible I would be tempted and fall in this way – the church would be half empty the following week once the congregation had heard the gruesome news. Numbers of people would feel bound to leave and no doubt some people's faith would be shaken (though they should never have been putting their faith in me, but God!). When you occupy a public position, be it spiritual or political, you have, whether you like it or not, a public persona. People believe your credentials as a minister of the Gospel, or as a politician, by the way you conduct yourself.

Nevertheless, despite being made a laughing stock, God forgave David instantly. We must realize that adultery is no more difficult to forgive than being a gossip. We have become experts at categorising sin and, consequently, dispensing "degrees" of forgiveness as a result. God does not view or handle our sin like that. God forgave David, but He did reveal the consequences that David would suffer as a result of his actions. The first was that he would never now build a temple for the Lord because he had blood on his sword. The second was that he would lose the child from this adulterous union. We can come back into the favour of God after committing sin, but it is always at a cost. The price of sin is that it often prevents us from fulfilling our potential. It stops us from getting to where we are meant to be in our destiny.

The covenantal aspect of sex

A few years ago, Jack Hayford wrote a book called *Fatal Attractions: Why Sex Sins Are Worse Than Others*[1] The strap line of the book seems to contradict my previous statement, yet I agree with what Hayford proposes. Sexual sins are "worse" than other sins in the sense that they have far-reaching emotional and spiritual ramifications for those involved. Sex is a sacred act intended to take place only within the safety and protection of marriage. When two people get married they make certain covenantal promises before God and sex is the seal, the physical signature, on that covenant. Their promises before God are not ratified until they have sex. That is why sleeping around and having sex with multiple partners is so devastating. From a spiritual point of view it means that effectively our souls are being "splintered" as we attempt to "covenant" with a number of people instead of just one as God intended. Man was never designed to function that way. Adultery is a violation of the spiritual covenant formed with your marriage partner. Even in a "post-Christian" nation like Britain, the law still stands that if a marriage has not been consummated then divorce is unnecessary – the marriage can be annulled. Even society recognizes that sex is the signature that validates the contract.

A girl once came to me and asked, "Can I get divorced? My husband ran off with another woman." I asked her, "Did they have sex?" "Yes," she replied. "Well, you can divorce him then," I told her. The act of sex outside of the marriage covenant breaks the covenant. Of course you can forgive that person and restore them and the covenant can be renewed. That would be the ideal, but it is not easy and not always possible. Some reading this will have suffered a marriage breakdown. For some, even though it wasn't their fault, the feeling of condemnation has not gone. But the Bible says, *"There is therefore now no condemnation to those who are in Christ Jesus, who do not walk according to the flesh, but according to the Spirit"* (Romans 8:1). If you have been the victim of adultery, you don't need to carry any guilt about it. Take your burden to Jesus and ask Him to deal with it.

In Ephesians 5 the apostle Paul uses marriage as the perfect "picture" to describe the spiritual covenant between Christ and His Church. Verse 23 states, *"For the husband is head of the wife, as also Christ is head of the church; and He is the Saviour of the body."* See the linkage: man and woman, Christ and the Church. Paul goes on to say,

> *"Therefore, just as the church is subject to Christ, so let the wives be to their own husbands in everything. Husbands, love your wives, just as Christ also loved the church and gave Himself for her, that He might sanctify and cleanse her with the washing of water by the word, that He might present her to Himself a glorious church, not having spot or wrinkle or any such thing, but that she should be holy and without blemish."*
>
> (Ephesians 5:24–27)

Paul then writes,

> *"So husbands ought to love their own wives as their own bodies;*
> *he who loves his wife loves himself. For no one ever hated his*
> *own flesh, but nourishes and cherishes it, just as the Lord does*
> *the church. For we are members of His body, of His flesh and of*
> *His bones. 'For this reason a man shall leave his father and*
> *mother and be joined to his wife, and the two shall become one*
> *flesh.' This is a great mystery, but I speak concerning Christ and*
> *the church. Nevertheless let each one of you in particular so love*
> *his own wife as himself, and let the wife see that she respects her*
> *husband."*   (Ephesians 5:28–33)

What Paul is saying here is that marriage is identical in nature to the relationship between the Church and her Groom, the Lord Jesus Christ. What this tells us is how seriously God views marital fidelity and therefore how seriously He views the sin of adultery. If marriage is a reflection of Christ and the Church, then how terrible to break that covenant and rip it apart.

Jesus on adultery

Paul pointed to the spiritual relationship between a man and a woman as they become "one flesh". Jesus, when it came to addressing the subject of marital infidelity also pointed to this "one flesh" principle. He did not, when questioned on the subject of divorce, refer back to the verses in Deuteronomy that speak about it, but instead spoke about the story of creation. Jesus referred back to Genesis 2:24 and pointed out that when a man loves a woman he will leave his parents' household, enter into a covenant with her and they will become one.

Jesus taught that once this "bonding" has taken place, a man and woman are permanently joined together. Older translations of the Bible talk about leaving and "cleaving" to become one flesh. To cleave means "to adhere to" which is where words like "adhesive" have their root. A married couple are literally "stuck" together!

Jesus picks up on this truth in Matthew 19:3–9 when a group of Pharisees come to Him and question Him on the topic of divorce:

> *"The Pharisees also came to Him, testing Him, and saying to Him, 'Is it lawful for a man to divorce his wife for just any reason?'*
>
> *And He answered and said to them, 'Have you not read that He who made them at the beginning "made them male and female," and said, "For this reason a man shall leave his father and mother and be joined to his wife, and the two shall become one flesh"? So then, they are no longer two but one flesh. Therefore what God has joined together, let not man separate.'*
>
> *They said to Him, 'Why then did Moses command to give a certificate of divorce, and to put her away?'*
>
> *He said to them, 'Moses, because of the hardness of your hearts, permitted you to divorce your wives, but from the beginning it was not so. And I say to you, whoever divorces his wife, except for sexual immorality, and marries another, commits adultery; and whoever marries her who is divorced commits adultery.'"*

Jesus was addressing a particular practice in Jewish tradition that men had abused and used as an excuse to treat women badly. Historically, men could simply turn to their wives and say, in effect, "I don't want you any more, go away." Moses introduced a letter of divorce in order to protect women and give them some rights in situations where marriages broke down. Jesus said, "Moses had to do that because your attitudes were wrong! You were hard-hearted." Then Jesus reveals the only situation in which God will allow divorce: "Anyone who divorces his wife, except for marital unfaithfulness, and marries another woman commits adultery."

Under Jewish law committing the sin of adultery normally resulted in death for the perpetrator. It would seem, however, that society at that time was so biased against women that it was nearly always women who were the accused and the ones "caught" in adultery and subsequently stoned to death. When I was a kid we had a saying: "It takes two to tango." When adultery occurs, no doubt one party was the first to instigate the event – somebody seduced somebody else – but ultimately, no one *had* to be seduced.

Why did Jesus see fit to mention adultery in the context of the Pharisees' question regarding divorce? Because He wanted to underline the centrality of the sexual union. The only thing which can cause divorce in God's eyes is the violation of the marriage covenant through the practice of illicit sex.

Jesus cited adultery as the chief reason for breaking the marriage covenant because marriage is the only covenant in the Bible that is sealed by sex. It is the most sacred personal transaction imaginable between a man and a woman. When a man and a woman have sex together a "soul tie" is created. In other words, a spiritual bond is formed between them that should never be broken.

In another confrontation with the Pharisees Jesus is "set up" by them in John 8:1–11. The scribes and the Pharisees bring to Him a woman "caught in adultery". As far as Jesus is concerned, these religious people's track record concerning adultery is so bad that He doesn't even look at them, He is busy writing something in the sand. I wonder what He wrote? Eventually, after the Pharisees badgered Jesus for an answer as to whether this woman should be stoned, He stood up, looked at them and said, in effect, "The one who has never lusted after a woman in his heart can cast the first stone." One by one the men skulked off and Jesus and the woman were left to speak.

> *"He said to her, 'Woman, where are those accusers of yours? Has no one condemned you?'*
>
> *She said, 'No one, Lord.' And Jesus said to her, 'Neither do I condemn you; go and sin no more.'"*   (John 8:10–11)

There has to come a time with our moral failure when God says to us, "I'll draw a line under it, but don't do it again." It has to be this way, otherwise we develop a philosophy that says, "OK, I can sin and do what I want to do and then come to God and say, 'Sorry!'" No, it doesn't work like that. That is premeditated sin and God does not tolerate premeditated sin. This provision is for people who have fallen and come back to God and say, "Lord, forgive me." God does.

There is another principle here that Jesus illustrates elsewhere in the Gospels, and that is, grace goes further than the Law. "The Law," Jesus says, "states, 'Do not commit adultery'." Then He goes a step further and says, "But I say, if a man has lusted after a woman, he has as good as done the act." Jesus' statement included 100% of men! Every man who has walked the earth, the only exception being Jesus Himself, has looked lustfully at a woman at one time or another. If you are reading this and you haven't then you probably need to book an appointment to see your doctor! I'm not letting women off the hook here though. Men, let's remember, are seduced by women, not by the television or magazines or the Internet. Over the thirty-five years that I have served as minister of our church, I have been propositioned a number of times, occasionally even before the service has ended! Lust is not exclusive to men – far from it. Men tend to have stronger sex drives than women, but women lust too, otherwise they would not be party to adultery. Unfortunately, many men are under the illusion that somewhere there is a married woman who wants to have sex seven days a week and this is what drives men to embark on adulterous relationships. The trouble is, such a notion is like the Holy Grail – it's a myth that someone invented!

On another occasion, Jesus was sitting by a well when an adulterous woman came to draw water. He knew full well, by the revelation of the Holy Spirit, that she had had a number of failed relationships and was now living with a man who was not her husband. But He didn't ostracise her as the Pharisees would have done, instead He sat at the well and chatted to her. She was a Samaritan woman and therefore an "unclean" foreigner who Jews would have avoided contact with. Most of the people of Jesus' day would have ignored her completely, but Jesus sits with her and says, "Can I have a drink?" What a God! Jesus demonstrated God's heart towards those who fail morally: compassion and the possibility of forgiveness. Jesus told the woman that the relationships she chased after would never satisfy her. Using the context of water, since they were seated by a well, Jesus pointed to Himself and told her that only the living water of God would ever satisfy the emptiness she felt inside. If she would allow God to touch her heart she could be forgiven and free. Jesus did not condone her behaviour, but He did not condemn her either. God wants us to know that there is never, ever, a level we can sink to where He cannot restore us.

To underline the fact that adultery has spiritual roots and is not merely physical, Jesus, in Matthew 12:39 spoke about "this adulterous generation". In this context Jesus was referring to those who would only believe God for His works and not His word. People wanted a sign from God before they would believe Him. Spiritual adultery, like physical adultery, is essentially selfish. We are adulterous when we want something from God but we are not prepared to give Him anything back. As adultery has become more "acceptable" in our society the sacredness of the sexual relationship has been lost and the prostitution of our sexuality has given place to a spiritual adultery so that we have become an adulterous generation.

Sadly, physical adultery is also prevalent among believers. There was a time when faithfulness to the family unit was the norm for Christians, but now this has changed. The University of Chicago conducted a national research poll survey only two years ago. They found that 25% of US men and 17% of US women admitted to being unfaithful in their marriage, which means 19 million men and 12 million women in the USA have committed adultery. Yet the figures amongst Christians were equally alarming. Out of 1,000 Protestant ministers who were anonymously asked if they had committed adultery, 300 of them admitted they had indulged in un-confessed adultery. Among Southern Baptist ministers 14% said they had slept with other women. And out of a Christian women's survey, 70% of the 1,000 women who were interviewed admitted to a relationship or intercourse with a pastor or a priest. When we lose the sense of our covenant with God and commit spiritual adultery, we lose it with each other!

Adultery-proofing your marriage

The best way of avoiding falling into the trap of committing adultery is to be proactive in protecting your relationship with your spouse. Remedial action will seldom be effective. Dr Willard E. Harley Jr., the psychologist, in his book *His Needs, Her Needs*[2] gave some useful advice on how to create a marriage that is characterised by faithfulness and not infidelity. Describing the married relationship in banking terms he says, "Your love bank for each other must never close." In any relationship we choose how much of a deposit we make into the other person's "account". How much we love our partner, how much we forgive them, are choices we have to make as an act of the will. No one wakes up one morning and suddenly discovers they don't love their spouse any more. It happens through neglect and through poor choices. Sometimes people don't keep their accounts topped up like they used to.

Harley helpfully lists what he sees as the five things that men need most from women, and women from men. Men and women both need different things from one another. Sadly, society has tried to merge and tamper with these differences. The world wants to feminise men and masculinise women! This is what Harley says that women most need from men:

1. Affection
2. Communication
3. Trust

4. Enough money to live on
5. For him to be a good father

A man needs:

1. Sexual fulfilment
2. Companionship
3. An attractive wife
4. Peace and quiet
5. His wife to be proud of him

King David could have blamed his adulterous relationship on his wife's lack of attention or the busyness of his role as king, but the fact is, as Psalm 51 recounts, he had to acknowledge that it was due to his own sin and impurity of heart. As St Augustine, one of the early Church fathers, wrote,

> "Passion is the evil of adultery. If a man has no opportunity of living with another man's wife, but it is obvious for some reason that he would do so if he could, he is no less guilty of it than if he had been caught in the act."

We are all guilty of adultery because we have all found another lover in our life at times apart from Jesus. It could be money, fame, business, people, but we have all been there and we all need to say, "God, forgive me. Restore me to the covenant of truth." God will forgive you and God will restore you. God is faithful. He is never adulterous. What God wants is for us to worship Him in Spirit and truth; to love Him with all our hearts and be faithful to Him and to the covenant of marriage.

The children of Israel were referred to on occasions as an "adulterous generation". Why? Because they were and are still a covenant people in relationship with Almighty God. History tells us that they often worshipped other gods, which in its spiritual dimension is equivalent to a physical relationship. They received forgiveness, however, when they showed sincere repentance and remorse for their sin. If you are the victim or the violator of such a covenant, know that healing and forgiveness is available from God for you.

Notes

1. Published by Regal Books, Ventura, USA, June 2004.
2. Willard E. Harley, *His Needs, Her Needs: Buidling an Affair-Proof Marriage*, Monarch, January 1986.

You Shall Not Bear False Witness

"You shall not bear false witness against your neighbour."
(Exodus 20:16)

This is the ninth commandment and in a sense one of the most difficult to address. The reason is simply that "bearing false witness" can operate on so many levels. If we think about committing adultery, it is fairly clear cut – we either have or we haven't. It is the same with murder – you either have or you haven't. But this commandment is harder to define and requires us to examine our heart and actions much more closely.

This does not mean, however, that we can take this commandment less seriously than all the others. It appears as an important part of the last six Commandments that are concerned with how we treat our fellow human beings. Bearing false witness is sandwiched between covetousness and dishonouring our parents, murder, adultery and theft. Breaking this ninth commandment can have just as serious consequences as we will see as we progress. I have witnessed firsthand the power of either keeping it or breaking it.

A lady came to me and told me the following story after I had preached on this commandment in our fellowship. She said, "A while ago I went through a season in my Christian life where I suffered from an extended period of mental illness. As you preached on bearing false witness and explained the different ways in which we do that to others, the pieces fell into place for me and I realized that what you were saying was absolutely true. I recalled having a big argument about something with my neighbours. We didn't part on good terms and they began bad mouthing me to other neighbours and I began bad mouthing them. Shortly afterwards I began to suffer from depression. During your message I realized that my attitude towards them was completely wrong and I immediately decided to stop cursing them. Instead, I began to bless them, pray for them and speak positively about them to others. Although they didn't change their attitude towards me, from that moment my health began to improve dramatically. I am now off the anti-depressants I was taking and am totally free from depression. Thank you for preaching that message. I know it is true!"

One might easily take this commandment to refer only to telling lies about someone – saying things that aren't true. But I believe its scope and depth are much greater than that. It includes not only making false oaths or promises that result in depriving another person of justice, but also "whispering", tale-telling, defamation, slander and anything that would conspire to injure a person, his character or his goods. It means all of that, as well as the obvious meaning of giving false evidence in court.

The value of a name

God saw fit to give us this commandment because the Christian faith, if it is based on anything, is based on the value of a name.

Hundreds of verses in the Bible speak about God's name. Psalm 113:2 says, *"Blessed be **the name** of the* L<small>ORD</small> *from this time forth and forevermore!"* Psalm 102:15 says, *"The nations shall fear **the name** of the* L<small>ORD</small>.*"* And, crucially, we read in Acts 2:21 that, *"Whoever calls on **the name** of the* L<small>ORD</small> *shall be saved"* (emphasis added). The name of God has value and it has power. God's name stands for everything He represents, everything He is.

In Western culture we don't place the same kind of importance on names as people do in other cultures. Africans think long and hard before naming their children. If you ask an African, "What's your baby's name?" it will always have a specific meaning like "Gift of God" or "Mighty Warrior". Jewish culture is also very conscious of names and how their meanings say something about the people who bear them. Jewish people, for instance, never call their children Caleb. Westerners do, simply because we identify with the heroism of Caleb in Scripture, how he went with Joshua into the Promised Land and was a man of great faith. Jews don't use the name simply because it means "dog"! Joshua means salvation and is a derivative of Jehovah, so Jews would use that name. The point is, their culture identifies more readily with *the name* than it does the person.

Jacob's name change

Jewish culture did not decide for itself that a person's name was so important. It came from God. It was important to Him and so it became very important to His people – an intrinsic part of their life and culture. A person's name can be immediately associated with their character and reputation. No one, therefore, wants to have a bad name, because it becomes a factor which limits us. God decreed that we should not denigrate one another's name because when a name becomes defamed and besmirched that name becomes synonymous with something bad.

One story stands out in the Bible with regard to having a bad name and that is the story of Jacob – the man who made a bad name for himself, but whom God acted graciously towards and gave a new name. Jacob is a nice name to give to your son, but the truth is, its meaning is not so nice! Jacob means "supplanter" or "deceiver". In other words, someone who steals from another. It can also mean "someone who belittles or defames others". Jacob was a supplanter because he conspired to cheat his brother out of his birthright and he did, in a very real sense, ruin his brother's name. Jacob deceived his father, robbed his brother and then absconded with his brother's birthright and his father's blessing. But he came to the point, as with everyone who acts falsely against another, where his actions rebounded on him. Esau, Jacob's aggrieved brother, tracked him down and inevitably their paths were bound to cross. Esau had gathered 400 men who were loyal to him and he was ready to attack and kill his brother for wronging him. Jacob was faced with a terrible predicament.

Sometimes it takes something to go wrong in our lives to drive us onto our knees before God. So often we go along in life oblivious of what we are doing and God has to allow something to happen in order to get our attention. How true this is of our violation of this commandment! Bearing false witness is something that has become ingrained in our culture. We are so used to doing it, at one level or another, that we hardly ever think about it. Do you ever indulge in a bit of gossip? Do you ever speak about people to others and say things about them or situations they are involved in when you don't really know all the facts? Do you listen to what people tell you about others and take what they are saying at face value without bothering to check out the details? We have all done these things and yet, even though they seem subtle infringements, we are bearing false witness.

Jacob, because of his predicament, was forced to come to God. There was no other way. He knew his brother was liable to kill him and he was in a real mess. We read in Genesis chapter 32 of the astonishing encounter he had with the Lord as he found himself literally wrestling with God.

> *"Jacob was left alone; and a Man wrestled with him until the breaking of day. Now when He saw that He did not prevail against him, He touched the socket of his hip; and the socket of Jacob's hip was out of joint as He wrestled with him. And He said, 'Let Me go, for the day breaks.' But he said, 'I will not let You go unless You bless me!' So He said to him, 'What is your name?' He said, 'Jacob.' And He said, 'Your name shall no longer be called Jacob, but Israel; for you have struggled with God and with men, and have prevailed.' Then Jacob asked, saying, 'Tell me Your name, I pray.' And He said, 'Why is it that you ask about My name?' And He blessed him there. So Jacob called the name of the place Peniel: 'For I have seen God face to face, and my life is preserved.' "*
>
> (Genesis 32:24–30)

What I find fascinating about these verses is the fact that, mid-wrestle, Jacob pauses to ask, "Tell me Your name"! The Lord replies, in effect, saying, "What's that got to do with you? This has got nothing to do with My name, but yours!"

What Jacob had done to Esau was to destroy his future. Esau would now never receive what was rightfully his by birth. But Jacob, through his actions, had also ruined his own name. In fact, he had lived up to his name – deceiver, supplanter. Jacob was seriously in need of a new name, otherwise his reputation would precede him for the rest of his life. And God in His mercy was gracious enough to give him a brand new name. But there was a consequence. The Lord put Jacob's hip out of joint and from then on he would walk with a limp – the sign of his sin but also of his redemption.

Why does God tells us this story? Because He wants us to know that what comes out of our mouth is of critical importance. God made us like Himself, in His image, and God's words hold creative power. When God speaks, things happen. In the same way, our tongues are a creative force. The words we speak can proclaim life or death over others. The apostle James had a great deal to say about our speech. James 3:6 records some of his incredibly strong words about the power of the tongue:

> *"The tongue also is a fire, a world of evil among the parts of the body. It corrupts the whole person, sets the whole course of his life on fire, and is itself set on fire by hell."* (NIV)

The truth is, what we say about another person can destroy them forever. They say that the pen is mightier than the sword. Well, the mouth is much mightier than the pen! There are people who have grown up hurting and dysfunctional simply because of the words others have repeatedly spoken over them. Think, for example, of the person whose parents, in a fit of rage, told them they were the result of a one night stand and were never really wanted. Or the person who was told, "We only planned to have two kids, you were an accident" or "you've been a pain in the backside all your life. I really wanted a son, not a daughter." Your parents may well have regretted saying such things. They may not even have meant them. But once they are out such words stay with a person for life. During the war a government poster featuring a pointing finger proclaimed the slogan "Loose talk costs lives." It still does.

Jacob called the place where he encountered God "Peniel" (literally "face of God"), *"For* [he said] *I have seen God face to face, and my life is preserved"* (Genesis 32:30, emphasis added). Here is a vital principle for us. God dealt with Jacob face to face. God never deals with anybody behind their back. God speaks to both His friends and His enemies face to face. If there is something wrong in your life, God will confront you about it. How we need to learn to do the same! How many times have we found ourselves discussing another person and suddenly they enter the room so we change the subject or go quiet?

It took a desperate struggle and resulted in a long-lasting injury before God was able to release Jacob from what he had done. Similarly, the consequences of what you say about a person has a lasting effect. Our words continue to echo long after the situation that caused them is over. Football fans will recall how David Beckham, probably the world's most famous footballer, was vilified both by fans and the media when he was red carded and sent off for violent conduct during England's match against Argentina in the second round of the 1998 World Cup. The match finished in a draw and England were eliminated in a penalty shootout. Many supporters and journalists blamed Beckham for England's exit from the Cup and he became the target of criticism and abuse, including the hanging of an effigy outside a London pub and a national tabloid newspaper printing a dartboard with a picture of him centred on the bull's eye. Beckham also received death threats after the competition. And we are talking about a single incident in a single game of football (albeit an important one to fans of the sport)! It took Beckham almost four years to find favour again with English football fans and re-establish his credibility.

Speaking falsely results in judgement

As Christians we need to be realistic about our definition of bearing false witness. The fact is, even if we don't directly speak lies about someone, if we persistently *listen* to other people judging, criticizing or slandering them, we are still as guilty as hell! The terrible thing is that by destroying the good standing and credibility of another, we bring judgement upon ourselves. When we allow our mouth to attack someone else's character we are also attacking ourselves. It happens even in church and I know of churches that have been destroyed, literally eaten alive from the inside out, by murmurings, groanings, stories, lies and gossip. The problem is, we are so vague about our definition of this commandment. If we truly recognized such activities as infringing God's law then we would be less inclined to do them. As it is we have an arsenal of excuses for what we do. "I'm just sharing this with you so you'll be able to pray intelligently . . ." or, with closer friends, "I wouldn't say this to anyone else, but . . ."

We are so deceived! If we do this we are making judgements about others and as a result we call judgement on ourselves. In Matthew 7:1–2 Jesus clearly states,

> *"Judge not, that you be not judged. For with what judgment you judge, you will be judged; and with the measure you use, it will be measured back to you."*

I believe that many people have no freedom in their life – their health, their finances – because they are continually speaking judgement on themselves by judging others. This habit we've gotten into is one of the main reasons why people leave churches and join different ones, and why some people have given up going to church at all. They see how hypocritical Christians can be! People are tired of hearing Christians bad mouthing one another. False witness is a cancer that is afflicting God's people.

False speaking was one reason that contributed to my own son leaving the church when he was eighteen. Now in his thirties, he has not been to any church since. Often he would overhear people speaking to me after a church service saying, "Fantastic sermon, Pastor Dave" and then hear those same people bad mouthing me during the week. My son, for all his faults, is a man of integrity, and he was disgusted that not one of those people who obviously had "issues" with me had the courage to come and speak to me direct. He could not resolve in his mind the conflict he witnessed and knowing that this type of Christianity was not for him, sadly he decided to leave rather than be a part of it.

Exodus 23:1–2 in the Amplified Bible says,

> *"You shall not repeat or raise a false report; you shall not join with the wicked to be an unrighteous witness. You shall not follow a crowd to do evil; nor shall you bear witness at a trial so as to side with a multitude to pervert justice."*

The New Living Translation puts it this way:

> *"You must not pass along false rumours. You must not cooperate with evil people by lying on the witness stand. You must not follow the crowd in doing wrong. When you are called to testify in a dispute, do not be swayed by the crowd to twist justice."*

It is clear from these verses that breaking this commandment begins with a whisper, a rumour, an allegation that is not accurate or true.

Once I had to take part in a television interview and found myself sitting next to an Australian psychologist who had just taken the post of head of a leading school of psychiatric medicine in London. He had spent a long time examining the findings of research carried out by his medical school to do with children who were sexually abused by their fathers. As you can imagine, it was a highly controversial, sensitive piece of work. After thoroughly investigating the findings of the report, this man was disturbed and he decided to re-interview the people whose case studies had been included in the report. He found that in most cases there had actually been no incidence of sexual abuse at all. The children had confessed, by auto-suggestion, that something had taken place because they found the situation intimidating and believed that it was what the interviewer wanted to hear. In most cases the fathers had done nothing and were innocent.

It was too late, however, to do anything about the devastating effect this piece of research had had on the families who had taken part. In most cases, despite the father being exonerated, the child's mother never accepted his innocence. Why? Because his good name had been brought into disrepute. Many men found themselves divorced and unable to visit their children, all because their names had been defamed and they were never forgiven for something they had not done.

That is the power of false witness, of putting somebody's name down. Once you have given somebody a bad name it is almost impossible to give them a good one back. That's why so often we see that when the press gangs up on a politician, more often than not they have to resign. It actually does not prove that they are guilty! It just proves that their name no longer has the credibility it once had.

Identity theft

In the Ten Commandments bearing false witness is immediately preceded by the commandment, "You shall not steal." I believe the two are closely linked. Bearing false witness is closely allied to stealing because, in a very real sense, it is "identity theft" – in this case the act of robbing someone of their good name and reputation. Bearing false witness wrecks a person's credibility and once that happens it is very hard for them to regain their good name. The apostle Paul in his letter to the Romans wrote,

> *"For the commandments, 'You shall not commit adultery,' 'You shall not murder,' 'You shall not steal,' 'You shall not bear false witness,' 'You shall not covet,' . . . are all summed up in this saying, namely, 'You shall love your neighbour as yourself.' Love does no harm to a neighbour; therefore love is the fulfilment of the law."*　　　　　　　　　(Romans 13:9–10)

Paul, like Jesus, taught that the Law could be fulfilled by embracing the concept of loving others. If we truly love other people, then we will not want to hurt and damage them. But, Paul says, if you are intent on despising your neighbour then bearing false witness against them is just as much a crime as murdering them! Jesus said that violating your brother with your mouth is no different to killing him.

Paul links obedience to the commandments with our spiritual wellbeing. He says in the following verse,

> *"And do this, knowing the time, that now it is high time to awake out of sleep; for now our salvation is nearer than when we first believed."*   (verse 11)

Paul says it is high time we woke up! He contends that if we persist in bad mouthing people, then spiritually we have fallen asleep. We are no longer alert and have dulled our spiritual senses. We need to wake up out of our deception and change our attitude. This is the one sin that is endemic amongst us all. We mask it by convincing ourselves we are "sharing" thoughts with one another or even sympathising over someone's condition. No, we are attacking their character! We are challenging people's decisions, but not to their face, which makes us at best cowardly and at worst an assassin. And if we take it too far, there is a law we can fall foul of where we can be sued for defamation of character.

The accepted legal definition of defamation is "the publication of a statement which tends to lower a person in the estimation of right-thinking members of society generally." The "statement" can be words, visual images or some other method of signifying meaning. Defamation takes two forms, libel and slander. Libel involves (amongst other things) writing or printing a defamatory statement. Slander is speech or gestures of a defamatory nature.

A lawyer in the US court case of Rosenblatt v. Bear (1966) summed up the position perfectly when he said, "The right of a man to the protection of his own reputation from unjustified invasion and wrongful hurt reflects no more than our basic concept of the essential dignity and worth of every human being – a concept at the root of any decent system of ordered liberty." In almost every case where a judge has ruled that words spoken or written about a person were defamatory, those words were directly attacking and denigrating the character of the plaintiff.

Paul knew about defamation more than anyone. He spent a great deal of time before he was saved destroying the character of followers of Christ. He knew, therefore, more than anyone why we should not do it. Paul tells us to wake up and stop sinning so that we don't end up like the foolish virgins of Jesus' parable, who had all the right trappings and looked the part, but who were spiritually dull. We need to wake up and smell the coffee! We can understand why the world bad mouths people – they don't know any different – but we should not do it.

Tackling the problem

So what steps can we take to tackle the problem? Here are four simple principles that I try to live by.

1. Follow the biblical pattern for conflict resolution

The Bible gives us a pattern for resolving conflict when we have a problem with another person. Instead of moaning to others behind a person's back we are to follow these simple instructions as laid down in Matthew 18:15–17.

(a) Go to the person and address the issue directly. I might add that we should do this with a measure of grace, not go charging in, throwing accusations around.

(b) If the issue cannot be resolved face to face, we are told to go back and take someone with us who can act as an arbitrator. This needs to be someone whom both parties will trust and listen to.

(c) If that doesn't work then we need to ask the person to go with us to speak to the church eldership so that they can make a judgement on the matter. If either party is unwilling to do this then it reveals that the problem is more deep seated than a simple disagreement or personality clash, as one or other of the parties is refusing to act in submission to biblical authority.

I have to say, I know hardly anyone who actually does that. All we hear is gossip and murmuring and it's all going on behind people's backs. People make the excuse, "I'm just giving my opinion on the matter." It's not an opinion, it's from the mouth of hell! You are destroying another person's character and they have no means of putting across their side of the story to the person listening to you. Jesus called it a curse. So did Paul. But we have imbibed it into our culture (as the proliferation of celebrity gossip magazines so easily demonstrates).

Christians should not behave like this. The Christian lifestyle is one that must be characterised by openness and honesty. Paul spoke from experience as a man who had had many believers imprisoned for their faith on false charges. He lied about them and listened to false rumours. He acted upon those allegations and reduced people's characters to shame. More than that he had people killed! It was only the grace of God that changed him. For some years many Christians could not trust him because he had bad mouthed them and because his own name carried a reputation.

2. Refuse to defend yourself

Years ago when people bad mouthed or criticised me I would go to great lengths to defend myself and would enter into long dialogues with people in order to exonerate myself. Now, I just tell myself, "If what they are saying about me is true then I'd better change. If it is not true, then forget it." The truth doesn't need defending. Someone once said, "If you are innocent, no defence is necessary, and if you are guilty, no defence is possible." If what somebody says about you is a lie, those who really know you won't believe it. And if they do believe it, then they didn't really know you in the first place! Your friends are those people to whom you *don't* have to say, "Honestly, I'm telling you the truth." They know when you are telling the truth and when you are lying. If you have to defend yourself to your friends, then they are not your friends. People like that are not friends, they're assassins with party hats on! True friends are those who are honest enough to tell you the truth when you mess up, but love you enough to do it in a non-condemning way.

3. Refuse to listen

In John 18 we read about the incident where Simon Peter denied knowing Jesus at His trial prior to His crucifixion. Peter stood at a distance, warming himself by the fire and some-one said to him, "Aren't you one of His disciples?" He denied it saying, "No, I'm not." This interesting situation shows that we can bear false witness by what we *don't* say, as much as by what we *do* say. Staying silent in a group of people when the character of someone you know is being questioned makes you as guilty as those who are gossiping. You may not go around deliberately bad mouthing people, but if you listen to it you are complicit. By your silence you are choosing to agree with it. When anybody comes to you with a loose tongue and makes an inflammatory statement about someone else, refuse to listen or you will be guilty as an accessory after the fact.

Earlier I mentioned that my son stopped coming to church because he could not abide listening to others attacking my character. To this day, even though he is not a practising Christian, he cannot abide hearing others defame another person's name and he has a method for dealing with it. He is gentle by nature, but strong in character. Usually he will get up and quietly leave the room, refusing to listen to what is being said. But if the gossip and slander continues he will confront the perpetrator and say, "Excuse me, you should not be talking like that about that person." He has even, at work, overheard somebody bad mouthing someone else to the boss and interrupted saying, "Excuse me, I know this is not my conversation, but he never said that because I was in the room at the time and I don't think you really mean to bad mouth that man, do you?"

If my son, who is not a practising Christian can do that, then God help us! How can I get my son back to church when most Christians wouldn't do what he does?

4. Always seek to resolve and never let things fester

There are some people who say, "I don't like confrontation" and for that reason refuse to deal with issues they have with others. Maybe they restrain themselves from gossiping about it, but they let it fester in their heart. Zechariah 8:17 cautions against doing this:

> " 'Let none of you **think evil in your heart** *against your*
>   *neighbour;*
> *And do not love a false oath.*
> *For all these are things that I hate,'*
> *Says the* Lord."   (emphasis added)

Whenever a problem occurs between us and another person we must always strive to resolve it because avoiding a confrontation and trying to bury it will only result in disunity in the church. Imagine the power of a church or community that had no gossip, no misinformation. If anyone wanted to discuss the personal actions of others we would refuse to listen and take that person directly to the one they had a difficulty with! Misquoting would be a thing of the past. A person's character would stand or fall by their own actions and we would not be living under the curse of limitation.

A self-survey

Ask yourself the following questions next time you start a conversation or are listening to one:

Q1: Is this conversation building somebody up or pulling somebody down? Some might object, "Aren't I entitled to my opinion?" According to God, no, you're not!

Q2: Have I spoken directly to the person concerned regarding this issue? If you have, then likely there is no need to be having a conversation about it with someone else. If you haven't, then you know you should take it up with them first and not talk to anyone else about it.

Q3: If the person walked into the room, would you or the other person talking to you be embarrassed? Or, would the person you are talking about be embarrassed if they came up behind you and overheard what you were saying? Think about how that person would react.

Q4: Are you misquoting or exaggerating the facts?

Q5: Is it your business anyway?

Q6: Would Jesus be saying it?

Q7: Would you like others to say exactly the same about you?

If you fall down on any of these questions then you are breaking this commandment! If you really want to go on with God then be honest with yourself and recognize that you fail in this area from time to time. Recognize too that all of us can live in obedience to this commandment regardless of our personality. Some make the excuse that they are just outspoken. In reality they're not – they are being unnecessarily offensive and defaming people without cause.

Every sin is bad, but I have seen so much perversion in our churches over the years through this sin that it will get me jumping up and down and hysterical every time. This is the little fox that ruins the vineyard. Bearing false witness is the virus that has infiltrated and killed church after church and is preventing revival breaking out in our nation. Let's make it our business to stamp it out!

You Shall Not Covet...

"You shall not covet..."
(Exodus 20:17)

A woman once reported to the Police that her husband was missing and had been gone for several days. The Police took a description of the man.

"Height?"

"Six feet four inches."

"Build?"

"Muscular."

"Hair colour?"

"Blond."

"Any other details that might be helpful?"

"Well, he's just a wonderful, lovely natured person, you know."

Looking totally perplexed, a friend who had accompanied the woman to the Police Station, protested, "What are you talking about? Your husband is nothing like that! He's short, chubby, bald and obnoxious."

"Yes," the woman countered, *"but who wants someone like him back?!"*

The truth is, in life we often set our hearts on something that we don't possess in reality. We look at what we've got, compare it to what others have, and then wish we had what they have! But in Exodus 20:17 God gives us the following commandment:

> *"You shall not covet your neighbour's house; you shall not covet your neighbour's wife, nor his male servant, nor his female servant, nor his ox, nor his donkey, nor anything that is your neighbour's."*

What does this old-fashioned sounding word "covet" mean? It means "to see and set your mind on something", to "set your heart on" or "to desire or long after". Covetousness is as old as sin itself. In fact one could argue that it was mankind's first sin. It was first manifest in the Garden of Eden and was the sin that the devil led Eve into, tempting her to covet the fruit which God had said was forbidden and causing her to lust after it. Eve succumbed because she coveted the "knowledge" she had been led to believe she would receive by eating the fruit. She made a choice, deciding that she wanted this thing that belonged to God more than she wanted to be obedient, wrongly thinking that possessing it would make her "complete" as a person.

William Shakespeare summed it up well when he said, *"Desire of having is the sin of covetousness."*[1] The Bible readily addresses the issue of desire. Paul tells us to *eagerly desire* the best spiritual gifts; to *desire* to hold the office of an overseer in the Church. These are good, positive things, so we know that "desire" in and of itself is not sinful. But covetousness is desire driven by *ungodly motives*. It is desire that does nothing other than feed our selfish nature. Covetousness is often accompanied by grasping actions or thoughts, either for that which we do not have and would like, or for that which belongs to someone else. It could be a relationship, a possession, even public acclaim and popularity. Whatever it is, covetousness desires to have that which does not belong to us.

The main trouble with coveting (and this is surely the reason why God gave the commandment) is that it so easily trips us up and leads us to commit other sins. Covetousness, I believe, contains the seed of *all* major sins. It is the seed which eventually grows into adultery, fornication, theft, loss of integrity and much more. The apostle James identified it as such when he said,

> *"But each one is tempted when he is drawn away by his own desires and enticed. Then when desire is conceived it gives birth to sin and sin when it is fully grown brings forth death."*
> (James 1:14–15)

James showed that the emergence of sin has a clear process and that process begins with ungodly desire – in other words, covetousness.

More than that, covetousness has a detrimental affect on other people, not just ourselves. When you have a covetous spirit towards someone you actually put limitations on them. For instance, if a person senses you covet something they have, they will become protective of it. Having sensed your envy they begin to behave differently. This might prevent them from telling you how God has blessed them, fearful of inflaming your jealousy further. It will eventually make that person instinctively hide things from you and suddenly they too are focusing unduly on this thing they possess that you want so badly. What has happened? Your covetousness has caused them to begin living in a place of restriction.

There cannot be a person alive who hasn't at one time said about his neighbours, "How can they afford a car like that? We can't! Why can't we have one like that?" We have all done it! The question I want to ask is, "What's wrong with the car you've already got?" The answer, most likely, is nothing. How readily we fall for the lie that having "better" things will make us "better" people or that having a better lifestyle will make us happier. They won't and it won't! The Bible calls it covetousness.

Not only did covetousness cause Eve to fall, it caused Cain to slay Abel, Jacob to live up to the meaning of his name: "supplanter", and there is perhaps no more terrible an example than that of King David and the incident with Bathsheba. We examined that story in detail in the chapter on adultery, but what was it that caused David's adulterous behaviour? Covetousness.

At the beginning of 2 Samuel chapter 11 we read that David happened to see Bathsheba bathing one night. He made a choice and instead of turning away and looking elsewhere he began to desire her. She was another man's wife but he coveted her and it led to conspiracy, adultery and finally murder – all because he wanted something that wasn't his. The irony is, David wasn't just any man, he was the king – the wealthiest man in the nation who could have literally anything he wanted. David could have taken any unattached, beautiful woman he wanted to be his wife, but he set his heart on having Bathsheba who belonged to another man. Covetousness is nothing to do with being poor!

David already had a beautiful wife. He did not *need* Bathsheba. But then covetousness is not about what we "need", it is about what we decide we "want". Covetousness is a sin of the eyes. We see something and then we decide, "I want that!" Have you ever watched children playing together? They can be playing quite happily until one child picks up a particular toy. Noticing this, another child, who wasn't even playing with the toy previously, will suddenly say, "I want that!" This child doesn't need the toy – there are lots of other toys – but something in him / her says, "I didn't want that until you had it, but I want it now!"

Looking at the issue of covetousness from a wider perspective you can see that covetousness at best is a selfish desire to have more material possessions in our life, but spiritually speaking it is a highly dangerous attempt by man to determine his own destiny in his own strength. What do I mean by this? Coveting is essentially man trying to get what he perceives he needs without involving or trusting God for those needs. By definition it is a rejection of trusting God to fulfil His destiny for you in His time.

In other words, God has a plan for your life. You can either trust Him to bring it about or you can try to take it for yourself through the sin of covetousness. It is man trying to manipulate his world in order to get what he wants. Yet covetousness will destroy everything we stand for if we allow it to grow in us. Look what it did to David. His lust led him to commit adultery with Bathsheba; he got her pregnant; the baby died; he had her husband killed. Those were the terrible consequences of his covetousness. Look what David then writes, referring to his sins, in Psalm 51:

"Have mercy upon me, O God,
According to Your lovingkindness;

According to the multitude of Your tender mercies,
Blot out my transgressions.
Wash me thoroughly from my iniquity,
And cleanse me from my sin.

For I acknowledge my transgressions,
And my sin is always before me.
Against You, You only, have I sinned,
And done this evil in Your sight –
That You may be found just when You speak,
And blameless when You judge . . .

Create in me a clean heart, O God,
And renew a steadfast spirit within me.
Do not cast me away from Your presence,
And do not take Your Holy Spirit from me."

(Psalm 51:1–4, 10–11)

This man was in a mess! All because of covetousness. This is what happens when you allow covetousness to eat your heart away.

Learning contentment

In Romans chapter 7 Paul, arguing about the Law, said,

> *"What shall we say then? Is the law sin? Certainly not! On the contrary, I would not have known sin except through the law, for* **I would not have known covetousness unless the law had said 'You shall not covet.'"**   (Romans 7:7, emphasis added)

It is interesting that Paul specifically picked covetousness out of all the potential sins he could have mentioned. Why not fornication, lying, stealing? I believe it is because Paul knew the seedbed of all other sins is covetousness; they arise out of the lust of the heart for something that is not ours by right.

Hebrews 13:5 says,

> *"Let your conduct be without covetousness, but be content with*
> *such things that you have, for He Himself has said, 'I will never*
> *leave you nor forsake you.'"*

As Christians, we should be content with whatever we have, because God has told us that He is aware of our needs and He *will* meet them. As children of God that is our promise. Therefore we need to learn to trust God because He is our source. Covetousness is nothing more than a deception. It robs us of trusting God by taking our eyes away from our Source and enticing us to find fulfilment in all kinds of things that will never satisfy or complete us. Covetousness sells us the lie that if we have "this" now it will make us happy, better, more fulfilled. Covetousness says, "I want that and I want it now!"

Abram fell into this trap. God gave him a destiny and promised him a son who would produce a nation. Abram was excited about this and he thanked God for it, but his wife, Sarai, was dubious. "Look at our age," she said. "We're sleeping single in a double bed. It's not going to happen, is it?" Sarai then said what no woman should ever say to her husband: "Have you considered my young maidservant?"! Abram replied, "Err, yes!" He didn't seem to argue a great deal about his wife's proposition! Covetousness kicked in and Abram tried to make the promise of God happen on his own terms and in his own way. Before too long a baby was on the way, but it wasn't the child of God's promise.

Needless to say, God wasn't pleased about this turn of events. Abram had succumbed to covetousness when he should have continued believing God for his destiny. God is not a liar. If He says He is going to bless you, then He is going to bless you. If God says He is going to give you something, then He will give it to you. It doesn't matter how long it takes, He will do it! You cannot live in your destiny if you are covetous. Jesus taught that we need to humble ourselves and submit to God in order to receive all we need, but covetousness takes the opposite approach. It grasps in order to obtain. Covetousness wants to claim for itself that which belongs to someone else without any sense of cost or commitment. It is self-appointed destiny by sinful means.

Covetousness is the thief of destiny. Destiny is taking hold of what belongs to us if we apply the principles that covetousness rejects. God has taught me this principle in my own life. He promised me, even though my background is that of an unlearned, uneducated man, that one day I would pastor a large church. As I write, every one of our Sunday services is packed out and we are busy building a 3,000-seat auditorium. It has taken thirty-five years for God's promise to begin to be fulfilled and there is still a way to go yet in terms of what God has promised me, but I can see the fulfilment of His promise taking shape. However, it has been vital for me not to try to bring about that destiny in my own strength and to not be covetous of what God is doing with anyone else.

As a young boy, living in a council house in Birmingham, unable to read and write, God came and spoke to me. He said, "Son, you are always coveting. You covet an education and many other things." It was true. I spent my whole life looking at other people and saying to myself, "I wish I was like them . . .

I wish I could do that . . . I wish I had what they have . . . " God by His grace spoke to me and gave me a destiny that meant I didn't have to covet any more. But it was clear to me that it would happen according to His timing and it would be achieved in His way. I'm sixty-one now and although God's promise has not yet been totally fulfilled, I can see God's destiny for me happening in front of my eyes. I am not panicking because of my age. I am content to trust God. He knows what He is doing.

People often come up to me and say, "It's great what God is doing through you. I wish I had what you've got." But they don't realize what they are asking for! By His grace, God is using me, but it has cost me thirty-five years of pain, rejection, misunderstanding, mistakes and regrets. Destiny wouldn't be destiny if it hadn't got those things in it! But covetousness has no substance to it except our own selfish desires.

No conception takes place in the heart when you are coveting something. All you have to do is dream about it and want it. By contrast, destiny has to have a conception; it has to germinate and grow. Achieving your destiny in life requires courage and commitment, whereas coveting wants to have the end results with no commitment. Courage and commitment are needed so that when things seem to be going wrong, we won't abort our destiny in God, but will hang on and believe Him to see us through. You can't just say, "I'll move on" when your destiny doesn't seem to be working out for you.

Paul said, *"I have learned to be content, whatever state I am in"* (Philippians 4:11). Notice that Paul had to *learn* to be content. Contentment is not a natural gift, but a discipline that has to be learned. It doesn't come naturally to us to be content when our friends are moving into a four-bedroom detached house and we are living in a three-bedroom semi. It doesn't come naturally to be content when our friend is getting promoted and we're not. It's not natural to be content when someone else is given a position we wanted. But, like Paul, we have to *learn* to be content so that we don't fall for the sin of covetousness.

Coveting doesn't cost a person anything. You can lie in bed and say to yourself, "I wish I had that house ... that car ... that job ... " This kind of thinking doesn't cost you anything (except that it robs you of reaching your potential). By contrast, living in your destiny can be quite costly, but the price is worth the reward. Over thirty-five years in ministry I have been through numerous trials and difficulties – too numerous to mention here! But the certain promise of God keeps me going forward. Often you have to be prepared to lay down what you've got and offer it back to God in order to receive it. Destiny people hold on to things lightly, but covetous people never let go of anything. By holding on and refusing to let go, the covetous person will lose the very thing God wanted to give them. Destiny people know that by letting go, they will be released to receive more of what God has for them. You have to learn to lay down in order to pick up.

Covetousness happens in the Church even among pastors. People ask me, "What car are you driving?" I tell them, "A four-year-old BMW." "Oh," they say, "I thought you would have had the latest with a church your size." Why? What would that prove? Do I have to have a big car because I've got a big church? The pastor who has his heart set on driving the best car has a covetous spirit and is teaching it to his people. We have to learn to be content whether we're given a Mercedes or the smallest car on the market. What does it matter as long as it gets us from A to B?

Let's not pretend that covetousness is not rife in the Church. Many people have said, "I should have been an elder ... I should be singing in the worship band ... I should have been running that ministry..." etc., even if it was only to themselves. Let's be honest, if we are not godly people we will even fight over who should be the next worship leader! We need to stamp out every occurrence of covetousness in our churches.

Combating covetousness

How do people find their way out of covetousness? There are a few lessons to learn:

1. Thankfulness

Very simply, if we are prone towards covetousness we are in the state we are in because we are in the state we are in! In other words, our covetousness is the very thing that is hindering us from progressing to the next stage in God's plan for our life. It is preventing us from moving forward and yet, if we did move forward we would find that we have no need to covet the things we've been coveting because God would provide for us! We need to learn how to move to the next level in life and the key to this is *thankfulness*. The paradox is, when you learn to be thankful to God for where you are now, then He can move you on to where you need to be!

2. Guarding your eyes

Covetousness, as we have already noted, is based on sight. It has to do with the "eye gate" of the body. You see things and want them, becoming jealous of those who own them. It might be a house you've seen, or someone else's wife or husband.

While covetousness is based on sight, destiny is based on *faith*. Covetousness has to do with the substance of things *seen* and hoped for. Destiny, through faith, has to do with the substance of things *unseen* and hoped for. It is important, therefore, that we consciously protect our eyes from leading us into sin. This requires self-discipline and practice, but it is possible for every person to guard their eyes and to avoid staring at those things that will give rise to covetousness.

Here is a simple test you can take in order to determine whether or not you have a tendency towards covetousness. Ask yourself the following questions:

Do I only speak or listen to people who have what I want, or do I take time with those who have little?

I understand the popular argument that if you want to achieve great things in life and if you want to learn, then you should associate with people who are themselves high achievers and who can impart something to you. But are you *only* found with people like this and no one else? Do you spend *all* your time around this kind of person? If so, it is probably because you are trying to live a life outside of who God has called you to be. There is nothing wrong in spending time with those who will stretch us, but we must also spend time giving input to people who can give us nothing in return. One preacher said, and I respect him for his honesty, that the reason he has nothing to do with me is because I am going in a different direction to him and I have nothing he needs that would warrant meeting me! Fair enough, but it made me think: how about giving something for a change instead of only taking? I believe that when you minister to people who have nothing to give you, God begins to entrust you with more and He also gives you the things that you need.

At Renewal Christian Centre we run a programme that provides food for single parents or families on very low incomes who are struggling. Some have asked, "How many people does that bring into the church?" But that is the wrong question to ask. We feed these people because they are hungry. We clothe them because they are naked. We visit them in prison or when they are sick because that's what Jesus told us to do! When I first came into ministry another pastor asked me what I most wanted to do and I said, "Become a hospital chaplain." He said to me, "Oh, that's a waste of time. Sick people won't fill your church!" "No," I replied, "but they'll fill the kingdom." Covetous people won't do things like this because there is nothing in it for them. We must position ourselves to minister to those who can do nothing for us in return.

Do I model myself on others, hoping to get what they have, or do I know who I am and live simply in obedience?

At times, do you find yourself behaving differently around different people? Or are you simply "you" no matter the setting or situation? When we first started our church and I was still in business, people had the wrong perception of me. They didn't realize that I came from a council estate. People would think, "We can't invite pastor Dave to our house for a cup of tea. We've got no furniture . . . the house is too shabby . . ." etc. So I used to call on people unannounced and just sit with them (sometimes literally on a box because some of our people were so poor) holding a chipped cup and have a cup of tea with them. People would say to me, "I never thought you would come to my house because we're so poor." I used to tell them, "If you're poor because you're bone idle, then get a job! But if you're poor because you've run out of money and you can't do anything else, let's pray about it." The point is: I set out to be myself regardless of people's perception of me. I didn't want to behave differently around different people. Nor did I want to model myself on others who were "successful". I just wanted to be who God had made me to be!

Do you rejoice when you see people receive what they have always wanted or are you resentful?

They say that a true friend is someone who applauds and cheers you on when you are doing well. A true friend does not resent your success, but celebrates it with you. We must be aware of saying, even to ourselves, "I wish God would do that for me."

Recently my wife and I moved house and it proved to be a somewhat traumatic experience. We had wanted to move for around five years and had looked at a number of houses but could never sell our house for some reason. Eventually we found a great bungalow which suited us and was approximately twenty minutes drive from the church (one of our criteria was that our house must be close to the church). The house was just outside Solihull where the church (and we) have been based for thirty-five years. We felt we had found the right place so we put an offer in and paid a deposit on the house. But as soon as we did that, a kind of grief came over me. I eventually realized it was a grief to do with leaving Solihull, the town that God called me to. In the end, Molly and I gave up that bungalow for a house just a few streets from the church that needed quite a lot of work doing on it.

Although I wouldn't say that we exactly "coveted" a nice little bungalow somewhere in the country, I suppose it was a dream. And yet, isn't it so much better to submit to what God wants and allow Him to put us where He wants us? When we cooperate with God's plan for us and refuse to covet we remain safe in the centre of God's will – the best place we can possibly be. When we covet we are being double-minded – trying to trust God and help Him along at the same time! Though at times it has been a struggle, like Paul, I have learnt to be content with what I have. We can choose to be people of destiny and allow God to bless us with what He wants in His own time and in His own way. But we need to keep our thought life in check so that we don't dwell on those things that God does not want us to have.

Jesus told a parable about a rich fool who suffered from the disease of covetousness. He was obsessed with growing his wealth so that one day he could live an easy life. Jesus, in His preface to this parable said, *"Take heed and beware of covetousness, for one's life does not consist in the abundance of the things he possesses"* (Luke 12:15). The character in Jesus' story planned to build bigger barns for himself to store the abundant crop he anticipated. His plan was to "eat, drink and be merry." But Jesus said,

> *"God said to him, 'Fool! This night your soul will be required of you; then whose will those things be which you have provided?' So is he who lays up treasure for himself, and is not rich towards God."*   (Luke 12:20–21)

Jesus taught that a man's blessing is not in what he can gather in this life, which he will ultimately be forced to leave behind, but in what he can take with him into eternity. The question is, what are you taking with you?

Consider the following statements and make a decision today that you will not live a covetous life.

- Covetousness has to do with self-will. Destiny has to do with God's will.
- Covetousness takes what has not been given. Destiny receives what has already been given.
- Covetousness exchanges eternity for time. Destiny submits time to eternity.
- Covetousness is the result of a rebellious spirit. Destiny is the reward of an obedient spirit.
- Covetousness has no assurance of the hand of the Almighty directing the feet of the righteous. It has no confidence that He, Christ, will supply all our needs according to His riches in glory. It is Abram taking a servant girl rather than taking Sarai, his destiny. It is Judas taking the silver when he could have had gold in Heaven.
- To covet is to consider the immediate gratification of self. Destiny is to consider the needs of others which brings peace to self.

Note
1. William Shakespeare, from *Twelfth Night*.

The Greatest Commandment

Loving God

Mark chapter 12 records a fascinating account of one of Jesus' many discussions with the scribes. The scribes were men whose primary occupation was writing out copies of the Jewish Scriptures and teaching people what the Law said.[1] They tended to be well respected in society for their literacy and knowledge because the teaching they provided formed the religious and moral backbone of the Jewish people. Because of their role they were often addressed simply as "teacher".

Jesus must have had numerous run ins with the scribes. Every time we read of such an encounter the scribes are questioning Jesus on His understanding of some difficult aspect of the Law. On the occasion recorded here in Mark 12 they had a question for Jesus regarding the resurrection. One of the scribes put a hypothetical scenario before Jesus:

> "Supposing a woman marries a man. They have no children and then the husband dies. As the law of Moses directs, the

*man's brother takes the woman as his wife, but subsequently he
dies too, so another brother from the same family takes his
place . . . "*

The scribes asked Jesus to imagine that this happened several
times in succession until all seven of the brothers in this one
family had married the woman and then expired! The woman
still remained a widow at the end. Their question to Jesus was,
"At the resurrection, whose wife will she be?" But Jesus
answered them,

> *"Are you not therefore mistaken, because you do not know the
> Scriptures nor the power of God? For when they rise from
> the dead, they neither marry nor are given in marriage, but are
> like angels in heaven. But concerning the dead, that they rise,
> have you not read in the book of Moses, in the burning bush
> passage, how God spoke to him, saying, 'I am the God of
> Abraham, the God of Isaac, and the God of Jacob'? He is not the
> God of the dead, but the God of the living. You are therefore
> greatly mistaken."* (Mark 12:24–27)

Jesus' response to the scribes was, in effect, "Actually, you are
missing the whole point because, experienced as you are in the
Scriptures, you have completely misunderstood them!" In
answering their question Jesus gave us a great insight into
eternity: there will be no marriage in Heaven (which, incident-
ally, scuppers a major doctrine of Mormonism). But Mark is
telling us this story in his Gospel because it is the precursor to
a much more important point that Jesus brought out of His
discussion with the scribes.

One of these teachers of Law, inspired by Jesus' answer

regarding the resurrection, raised another issue – one which is significantly more fundamental to life:

> *"Which is the first commandment of all?"* (Mark 12:28)

Or as the NIV translation puts it:

> *"Of all the commandments, which is the most important?"*

This man wanted to hear what Jesus had to say about the Law as a whole. What, in Jesus' opinion, was the pinnacle of God's law? Jesus answers the man with a statement that is not actually one of the Ten Commandments. He says,

> *"The first of all the commandments is: 'Hear, O Israel, the LORD our God, the LORD is one. And you shall love the LORD your God with all your heart, with all your soul, with all your mind, and with all your strength.' This is the first commandment. And the second, like it, is this: 'You shall love your neighbour as yourself.' There is no other commandment greater than these."*
> (Mark 12:29–31)

The first part of Jesus' answer was a recitation of Deuteronomy 6:4–5. This became known as the *Shema* and is still viewed as the most important prayer in Judaism, being recited twice daily. In this amazing statement Jesus exposes the heart of real faith – to love God wholeheartedly and to love others with the love of God. Mark 12:32–34 records the response of the scribe who asked Him the question:

> *"The scribe said to Him, 'Well said, Teacher. You have spoken the truth, for there is one God, and there is no other but He. And*

*to love Him with all the heart, with all the understanding,
with all the soul, and with all the strength, and to love one's
neighbour as oneself, is more than all the whole burnt offerings
and sacrifices.' Now when Jesus saw that he answered wisely,
He said to him, 'You are not far from the kingdom of God.' But
after that no one dared question Him."*

Why did the scribe ask Jesus this question? What was his
motivation for doing so? My theory is that this man, despite
his vast knowledge of God's Word, was still searching for the
answer to the question that had plagued him for years: "How
does a person really know for sure that they have eternal life?"
This man was probably a decent, God-fearing, religious man.
But for all that, he had not yet discovered the truth. Jesus
describes him as being "not far" from the kingdom of God – but
he had not yet received the full revelation he needed in order to
have assurance of eternal life.

Most people, whether they acknowledge it openly or not, are
asking that same question: "If there is a God, how do I find
Him?" or, "If there is an afterlife, what happens to me when I
die?" Those are reasonable questions that every person needs to
ask themselves because there will come a time when every one
of us leaves this life. Questions regarding our eternal destiny
need to be settled on this side of eternity. It's no use getting on
an aeroplane and then asking, "Where is this flight going?" is it?

Jesus answered the scribe by quoting two commandments,
yet notice that He linked them together: the loving of God is
connected with the loving of others. One automatically leads
to the other. So Jesus' statement illustrates a very important
principle to us: obeying the second part of this commandment
is unworkable if we are not obeying the first part. In other

words, we will never truly love others (or ourselves) if we don't love God wholeheartedly.

Motivated by love

Christianity is the only faith that has a God of love.

Recently I took part in a radio programme and a young Muslim lady was on after me. During her broadcast she told the interviewer, "I'm doing my best to please God." It reminded me of the fact that "religion" (as opposed to a relationship with God through Christ) is all about trying to please or appease God and gain His approval by our actions. There are ninety-nine names for god in the Muslim faith, but "love" is not one of them. Yet, at the very centre of the Christian faith is the greatest commandment which, Jesus says, is all about LOVE. Imagine a marriage in which a woman "does her best" to please her husband all the time and spends all her time "trying to keep him happy". Where is the relationship in that? God does not expect us to relate to Him like that. He wants to have a two-way relationship with us because He is a God of love.

The whole concept that makes Christianity so different from every other faith is that its foundation is a love relationship with a loving God. God loved us even before we had a clue who He was! Love caused Him to sacrifice His Son for us when we didn't care less about Him! Because a two-way relationship is the heart of Christianity we don't have to try to appease God. We don't have to get up in the morning and offer Him sacrifices or bring Him fruit so that He won't send lightning, floods or some other disaster on us! He is a God of love, not vengeance. Understanding this commandment is the key to living a successful Christian life. If you can crack this one then you are untouchable!

The Amplified Bible renders Deuteronomy 6:5 the verses like this:

> *"And you shall love the Lord your God with all your [mind and] heart and with your entire being and with all your might."*

Loving God is an act of the will, it takes some effort. But when you surrender your whole being to God – body, soul and spirit – there are untold benefits. God blesses, strengthens and renews us. How many of us know that when a man is in love with a woman he thinks nothing of travelling hundreds of miles to see her? He finds the physical resources to do what he is motivated to do. In other words, his body comes into submission to his love. When I was dating Molly I would often deliberately miss the last bus home just so I could have another ten minutes with her. It meant I would then have to walk five miles to get home, but I did it – even in the snow – because I was motivated by love! Love motivates you physically, mentally, emotionally and spiritually.

Our response to God's love

I serve as one of the governors of a school in our area and I was asked by my fellow governors if I would oversee the area of discipline in school life. We have put in place all kinds of systems to help kids who are getting into trouble and also seek to support their parents as much as possible, but I am not soft on the kids I meet during disciplinary meetings. Recently, I said to one boy, whose mother constantly cried throughout the meeting, "You don't love your mother!"

Shocked, the boy responded, "Yes I do!"

"No you don't," I responded. "because if you did then you would not be breaking her heart by behaving in this way!"

Love must produce action!

Just as when someone offers us something to eat, we respond, or if someone offers us money, we respond, God loves us and we must respond to Him. God offers us a two-way love relationship that will utterly transform who we are – but we have to respond to Him first in order to partake of it. The act of loving God triggers the beginning of our transformation.

When Peter was chosen to be the founder of the Church, Jesus didn't ask him, "Can you speak in tongues, Peter?" or "What are your views on eschatology?" He didn't ask about Peter's (nonexistent) theological training. Jesus simply wanted to know, "Do you love Me?"

Initially Peter could not respond to Jesus to the depth that Jesus required. An examination of the Greek text reveals a conversation that went something like this:

"Peter, do you love Me?"

"Lord, I'm very fond of You."

"But, do you love Me?"

"I can't think of anyone else whose friend I would rather be."

"Yes, but do you *love* Me?!"

Finally, Peter responds, "Yes Lord, as much as I can."

Jesus stepped down to Peter's level and became the friend of a man who could not love Him until he had had a spiritual experience on the day of Pentecost. That day the Holy Spirit came upon Peter and God's agape love flowed through him for the first time. Peter was transformed from being a man who wasn't able to stand by Jesus on the day of His arrest and denied

Him three times, into a man who, tradition has it, was crucified upside-down because he said, "How can I be crucified in the same way as the one who loved me unto death?" Only the love of God can do that!

Similarly, Paul allowed himself to be beaten when as a Roman citizen he didn't need to be! But he took it for the sake of the Gospel. His identity was found in Christ, not in his Roman citizenship. He preached Christ tirelessly because he was motivated by the love of God. In Romans 8 Paul wrote about being *"more than conquerors through Him who loved us."* According to Paul, the power that delivers us from all the attacks of the enemy is the love of God. Our victory in life comes out of our love relationship with God. The extent of our victory is very much dependent on the depth of our response to God's love. This is the secret of Christian living: we respond to God's love, we avail ourselves of His forgiveness, we accept His mercy and His grace. Unless we have had a supernatural encounter with the living God we can only become "good" people not "God-people".

Joshua 22:5 says,

> *"Take careful heed to do the commandment and the law which Moses the servant of the* LORD *commanded you,* **to love the** LORD **your God,** *to walk in all His ways, to keep His commandments, to hold fast to Him, and to serve Him with all your heart and with all your soul."*   (emphasis added)

We are commanded to love God. If Jesus commands us to do it, it means that (a) it is possible, and (b) it begins in our will. Love is a choice, a decision, a response. We love God because He first loved us.

Loving ourselves

If our God is a God of love, and if love is central to Christianity, why is it that so many people fail to love themselves? It appals me that so many people in the Church have such low self-esteem. How can that be when God's essence is love?

Many of the statements we hear Christians making about themselves are utterly irrelevant in the context of our loving God and they reveal a deep misunderstanding of His nature. How often do we hear people say, "I don't know how God can love me" or perhaps, "I don't know how God can forgive me after what I've done." Do people realize that making such statements is tantamount to saying, "I don't know God!"? If we have no knowledge of the love of God in our lives, which brings an incredible sense of self-acceptance and belonging, then we really don't know God that well.

Yet, our churches are full of people who, according to Jesus, don't act like Christians because they do not love themselves. They put themselves down all the time, they don't like themselves, they persecute themselves and they think that nobody cares for them. They have simply not embraced the love of God that is found in Christ. When you understand and accept God's love for you, you begin to understand how He sees you, and this revelation changes you forever! God does not see you as a failure. He loves and accepts you and He wants you to understand that.

Imagine a couple who have recently been married. The woman was married previously but was abused by her husband constantly. Imagine how hurt her new husband would be if his wife only ever talked about how bad her previous husband was and never mentioned or appreciated how great he, her new husband, is. It is the same with God. When we come to Christ and are brought into the love of God, how sad to spend all our time talking about how unworthy and useless we are. God wants us to appreciate the fact that we are now forgiven, loved, accepted. Personally speaking, I had a disastrous upbringing, but once I realized that God loved me and could put His love inside me, it utterly transformed me!

The devil, of course, constantly comes to us and says, "Why should God love *you?*" and points to all the dreadful things we have done in our lives. We must not believe this lie. Whenever he does this a good response is, "Why shouldn't God love me?" Think about it – why *shouldn't* God love you? He should, because *He is love!* The day God doesn't love you is the day He denies His own nature. If we don't respond to God's love we are rejecting who He is. If we don't begin to love ourselves we reject who He is. I'll put it even more strongly: to not love yourself when God loves you is an act of rebellion against the gospel of Christ!

If only the Church would grasp this message and believe it we would not find ourselves constantly fire-fighting, ministering to Christians with low self-esteem and self-worth who are broken, hurt and rejected. Neither would we have so many people walking out of churches because others have offended them (in other words, dented their already low self-esteem). Instead, secure in ourselves in the love of God, we would deal with any issues that come up and learn that love keeps no account of wrongs, but covers a multitude of sins.

Years ago I was a very insecure person because I could not read or write. I had an uncontrollable temper. I was unforgiving and foul-mouthed and the reason for this was simply that I didn't love myself. Whenever you encounter a person who speaks negatively, criticizes others often and is foul-mouthed or abusive, they are always telling you more about themselves than their problems! Loving yourself in the love of God transforms you. It transforms the way you think, the way you talk, the way you conduct yourself. Forget about "Woe is me, I don't know why God loves me." If Christ died for you, then you are worth something!

It is impossible to know and experience the love of God and not have your self-worth restored and your self-esteem raised. Self-love is the result of God's love as He invades our spirit with His wellbeing. I often counsel people who say to me,

"Pastor Dave, nobody loves me."

"I do," I tell them.

"Oh, I know *you* do!" they say.

"... And your husband/wife does."

"Yes, I know *they* do ..."

Usually when people say things like this they are looking for endorsement, affirmation. They don't truly believe that "no one" loves them. So often we look to others to ascribe value and worth to us when only God can do that effectively. When we have experienced the vast reservoir of God's love and mercy we can never be the same again. All false humility is drowned in the flood of His love. God's redeeming love eradicates the "poor me" syndrome.

I have a healthy respect for all that God has done for me and in me and will do. I am what I am by the grace of God. How can we not love what God loves? How can we not forgive what God has already forgiven? How can we not value what God calls precious?

Moses' story

When Moses encountered God he was an old man of eighty and he stammered. Moses had no self-confidence at all. God told him that He was going to use Moses to lead a million people out of Egypt, releasing them from the oppressive regime of Pharaoh. Moses was stunned. How could he, weak as he was, do such a thing? But God, of course, was serious. He never sets us up for a fall and He never humiliates or embarrasses us. He never asks us to do something He knows we cannot do. In Exodus 3:11 we read how Moses protested.

> *"Moses said to God, 'Who am I that I should go to Pharaoh, and that I should bring the children of Israel out of Egypt?'"*

Why is Moses saying, "Who am I?" It wasn't him who had to bring the people out, but God! God reassures him, but in Exodus 4:1 Moses asks another question:

> *"But suppose they will not believe me or listen to my voice; suppose they say, 'The LORD has not appeared to you.'"*

So God did a miracle with Moses' staff to prove to him that He would be there in power, supporting him every step of the way. But Moses had a third objection:

> *"O my Lord, I am not eloquent, neither before nor since You have spoken to Your servant; but I am slow of speech and slow of tongue."*   (Exodus 4:10)

God patiently replied,

> *"Who has made man's mouth? Or who makes the mute, the*
> *deaf, the seeing, or the blind? Have not I, the* Lord*? Now*
> *therefore, go, and I will be with your mouth and teach you what*
> *you shall say."*   (Exodus 4:11–12)

Moses, however, still had zero confidence and self-esteem! He
still tried to squirm out of what God was asking him to do:

> *"O my Lord, please send by the hand of whomever else You may*
> *send."*   (Exodus 4:13)

By now God was fed up with Moses' stubborn refusal of His
calling and offer of love and support. God was angry. He was
angry because Moses did not trust Him. When you love people
you trust them. You trust them to take you places and not
abandon you, to carry you and not drop you, to walk with you
so you don't get lost. Moses didn't know how to trust God at
first, but over the years God's love transformed him. He
changed from being self-reliant to God-reliant. He was formerly
a self-centred, inadequate man, but he became the man whom
God called his friend.

We too are God's friends:

> *"Behold what manner of love the Father has bestowed on us,*
> *that we should be called children of God! Therefore the world*
> *does not know us, because it did not know Him. Beloved, now*
> *we are children of God; and it has not yet been revealed what we*
> *shall be, but we know that when He is revealed, we shall be like*
> *Him, for we shall see Him as He is."*   (1 John 3:1–2)

And Jesus said,

> *"As the Father loved Me, I also have loved you; abide in My love.*
> *If you keep My commandments, you will abide in My love, just*
> *as I have kept My Father's commandments and abide in His*
> *love."*   (John 15:9–10)

If we abide in God's love we can continue strong – even when we go through very difficult times. Through trials and tribulation may come, we don't need to doubt our identity and security as sons and daughters of God because God's love is a constant, unchanging factor in our lives.

Loving Others

1 John 4:8 says (very bluntly),

> *"He who does not love does not know God, for God is love."*

Just stop there! Christianity is a bit more serious than we thought! When John says "He who does not love . . ." here, he is referring to loving others. Jesus has commanded us not just to love God, not just to love ourselves, but to love others also – and not just those people we like or our family, but everyone! "Wow!" you may say, "That's hard! There are some people who I just can't love."

Of course we cannot love everyone *in our own strength*. But with the transforming power of God at work in our lives we *can* love others. The Bible makes it clear that we don't love God, ourselves and others out of our own effort, but *as a direct result* of receiving God's love for us:

> *"In this is love, not that we loved God, but that He loved us and sent His Son to be the propitiation for our sins. Beloved, if God so loved us, we also ought to love one another . . . If we love one another, God abides in us, and His love has been perfected in us."*
>
> (1 John 4:10–12)

It is out of the overflow of God's love in our life that we find ourselves able to love and accept ourselves for who we are, and in turn, to love and accept others for who they are. The fuller we are with God's love, the easier we will find this task.

Love your neighbour?

In the Old Testament a respect for one's neighbour was taught so that society would have order and harmony, but Jesus took this command to a totally new level when He taught it as part of the Beatitudes:

> *"You have heard that it was said, 'You shall love your neighbour and hate your enemy.' But I say to you, love your enemies, bless those who curse you, do good to those who hate you, and pray for those who spitefully use you and persecute you, that you may be sons of your Father in heaven; for He makes His sun rise on the evil and on the good, and sends rain on the just and on the unjust. For if you love those who love you, what reward have you? Do not even the tax collectors do the same? And if you greet your brethren only, what do you do more than others? Do not even the tax collectors do so? Therefore you shall be perfect, just as your Father in heaven is perfect."*
>
> (Matthew 5:43–48)